THE COMIC VISION IN LITERATURE

THE COMIC VISION
IN LITERATURE

Edward L. Galligan

The University of Georgia Press   Athens

© 1984 by the University of Georgia Press
Athens, Georgia 30602

Illustrations by G. D. Davidson

Designed by Sandra Strother Hudson
Set in Linotron 202 10 on 13 Times Roman

The paper in this book meets the guidelines for
permanence and durability of the Committee on
Production Guidelines for Book Longevity of the
Council on Library Resources.

Printed in the United States of America

88   87   86   85   84   5   4   3   2   1

Library of Congress Cataloging in Publication Data

Galligan, Edward L.
The comic vision in literature.

Includes index.
1. Comic, The.   2. Wit and humor—History
and criticism.   I. Title.
PN6147.G34   1984   809'.917   83–18205
ISBN 0–8203–0713–0 (alk. paper)

For my mother and my father,
who taught me to trust in love and delight in laughter

CONTENTS

PREFACE

Like everyone else who has ever written about comedy I have had trouble with terms since the minute I started working on the subject. By its nature the subject will not yield to clear, precise terminology; instead one must use familiar but hazy terms carefully, hoping that they will gradually become reasonably clear. When worst comes to worst, one must borrow or concoct unfamiliar terms, hoping that they will point with reasonable clarity toward the significance of matters that are rarely dealt with in words.

The difficulty begins with the term *comedy* itself. Any generally acceptable definition must be exceedingly broad and vague, for the good reason that people have found it necessary to use *comedy* and its derivative *comic* to refer to an extraordinarily wide variety of works and acts occurring in almost every known human society and even among some animal groups. (Apes, too, have their jokes.) Some literary critics have reacted against that vagueness by defining comedy as a literary form, usually as a drama. Mostly they have been heavily influenced by Aristotle's *Poetics* and see themselves as applying Aristotelian methods to achieve Aristotelian clarity, but the more rigorously they apply these methods the more preposterously circumscribed become their results. Define comedy as drama and it immediately becomes impossible for you to discuss or even think about works in other forms, even works that have been heavily influenced by drama, such as the novels written by Henry Fielding after his years as a playwright. Define comic drama rigorously and you are left with only a small number of plays written in a few scattered periods of Western history that are entitled to the name of comedy. Clarity is a desirable quality to discover in a piece of criticism, but there is a limit to the price one can afford to pay for it. Preferring to risk getting lost in the fog of a broad, loose definition, I assert that comedy is a mode of the imagination, manifested in all of the forms and ways the imagination expresses itself. Accepting that, I have moved slowly to accumulate an understanding of the mode, comparing this work with that one, looking for marked similarities and for recurring symbolic gestures, never quite certain of the adequacy of my way of stating them, but finally sure that some coherent system of attitudes and values underlies the mode. There is such a thing as a comic vision of reality, which is every bit as concerned with issues of fundamental importance as the tragic vision; we are obligated to attempt to understand and, I think, to heed it.

But finding terms for developing and conveying an understanding remains a difficult, stubborn problem. To take a simple yet annoying example, I am convinced that gaiety is both the greatest virtue known to the comic vision and the most profound reward of comic works, but the gaiety of comedy has little to do with the gayness of politically concerned homosexuals. The term has been so muddied for us by those political battles that I would avoid it if I could. I cannot; it is irreplaceable. All I can do is use it and trust that my readers will understand it clearly in the traditional sense. In other, more complex matters no such straightforward solution is available. For example, *ideas* is a misleading term to use in connection with comedy's significance; *images* is better, but I use it reluctantly and warily. I find myself in more difficulty as I try to find words to identify some of the most fundamental of the images, such as comedy's image of will or its image of order.

Comedy distrusts assertions and explanations and delights in gestures. Assertions and explanations are attempts to make words mean *this,* not *that;* comedy prefers to celebrate both *this* and *that* as simultaneously as possible. Thus, the classic conclusion of a comedy is pure gesture, a dance or a ceremony, but even comedies of a non-classical character will end in a symbolic gesture rather than a summary assertion. The conclusion of *The Adventures of Huckleberry Finn* is a gesture, Huck's decision "to light out for the Territory," and a hundred years later we are still debating its exact significance. In general, comedy's way with words is gestural rather than logical, doubling their meanings rather than simplifying them. One can see this even in a joke so simple that it was stale the day after it was first

PREFACE

used (probably in a nineteenth-century minstrel show): "Who was the lady I saw you with last night?" "That was no lady, that was my wife." *Lady* and *wife* are both doubled terms, for the second man is both complaining that his wife is not ladylike and bragging that she is a real wife, part of a relationship too powerful to be constrained by the rules of genteel behavior.

For further, much more complex illustrations one can go to the films of W. C. Fields or the poems of E. E. Cummings: "I will bend every effort, and I come from a long line of effort-benders," says Fields in *Tillie and Gus;* "what if a much of a which of a wind," sings Cummings at the beginning of one of his most characteristic lyrics. Or consider Mollie Bloom's superbly encompassing reiteration of the words *and* and *yes* at the end of *Ulysses.* Even George Bernard Shaw, who appears to be the most fiercely wordy of comic artists, pulls the rug out from underneath his words at the end of *Man and Superman* when Ann Whitefield says to Jack Tanner, "Never mind her, dear. Go on *talking.*" Anyone attempting to deal in the language of criticism with an art so deeply gestural must proceed cautiously, tentatively, like a man crossing a stream on a footbridge that may or may not be sound.

Comic art, like all other kinds of art, speaks to and for all of us in every recess of our lives, and the comic vision is possessed by ordinary, uncelebrated men and women as well as great artists. One can see it in small matters and large, in the shrug of the shoulders of somebody discovering that yet another lottery ticket is a loser and in the teeth-gritting grin of the patient who refuses to give in to self-pity even though the doctor has just delivered the worst possible news. Comedy is often funny, but it is never merely funny: it is *about* something. Comedy concerns those life and death matters that all of us must cope with through most of our lives—sex and dying, aggression and injustice, love and vanity, rationality and sense. In this book-length essay I describe *some* important aspects of the comic vision and identify *some* of its imperatives. I cannot possibly be comprehensive: the works of the comic vision are innumerable and its imperatives are subtle and complex.

PREFACE

I begin where I am convinced any critical consideration of comedy must begin, with a discussion of the theory of jokes. I work with the theory that Arthur Koestler elaborated in *The Act of Creation* and other books. It is the best—the soundest, clearest, most helpful— theory that I know. It firmly connects joke-making to the highest forms of creativity, and it explains, as other theories do not, several of the most glaring truths about humor. It also meshes with William Lynch's theory of comedy, which I discuss in my second chapter. These two theories mesh so completely that each supports and con- firms the other, even though Koestler was a wholly secular man and Lynch is a Jesuit theologian and neither appears to have read the works of the other. Comedy does delight in making odd bedfellows.

The remaining four chapters and the coda will be much less the- oretical as I apply ideas arising from the theories to a number of different works of comic art written in various times, places, and forms. Rather than survey all of the important works of comic liter- ature I choose for discussion those works that have struck me as revealing with particular force and clarity some important charac- teristics of comedy. The absence of other writers or works from the discussion implies nothing whatsoever about my judgment of their importance. I have little to say about Chaucer or Rabelais, but I am not so insensitive as to value them lightly. I do value highly the works and writers I discuss, if only out of gratitude for what they have shown me; however, in most instances—for example, Cer- vantes and Mark Twain—these judgments are unexceptionable. If a few are somewhat surprising—Heinrich Böll and Georges Simenon— I argue that they are so only because these writers and their books have been improperly neglected by American criticism, which, like the criticism of other nations, is sometimes parochial and often faddish.

The comic vision forces those who are faithful to it to acknowl- edge that they are themselves part of what they laugh at. This is as true for critics as it is for comedians, though critics are excused, thank heaven, from any obligation to be funny. Critics who do not acknowledge that the rationality and willfulness on which their crit- ical assurance is based are part of the rationality and willfulness that comedy mocks are deluding themselves and trying to delude their readers. That is why this book is written in a style much more informal than that of critical works dealing with sober subjects: the prose must avow that the critic is an ''I,'' full of the uncertainties and idiosyncrasies that the personal pronoun implies, too undignified to be labeled ''the author,'' and too brash to shelter behind passive constructions. The writer of this book is a fool in various ways, but so, of course, is his reader. That is an example of what the comic vision does for us; it relieves us of the need to pretend to be more than we are and thereby frees us to make the most of what we are and have. In the words of the comic master of Walden Pond, ''any truth is better than make-believe.''

ACKNOWLEDGMENTS

I n the course of writing this book I have drawn in varying degrees on published pieces of mine and I am grateful to the editors concerned for permission to quote from these works: "Intuition and Concept: Joyce Cary and the Critics," *Texas Studies in Literature and Language* (Winter 1967); "Simenon's Mosaic of Small Novels," *South Atlantic Quarterly* (Autumn 1967); "The Comedian at Walden Pond," *South Atlantic Quarterly* (Winter 1970); "The Usefulness of Arthur Koestler's Theory of Jokes," *South Atlantic Quarterly* (Spring 1976); "True Comedians and False," *Sewanee Review* (Winter 1978); "William Lynch's Theory of Comedy," *South Atlantic Quarterly* (Spring 1978); and selections from the Introduction to *A Choice of Days* by H. L. Mencken. Copyright © 1980 by H. L. Mencken Estate. Reprinted by permission of Alfred A. Knopf, Inc.

I am also grateful to the Faculty Research Fund of Western Michigan University for two grants in support of this project.

1.
A
THEORY
OF
JOKES

L aughter is a test for and of jokes. If a gesture or utterance causes someone to laugh, it is a joke, at least for that person. If it causes a number of people to laugh, you must concede that it is a joke even if you do not laugh yourself. If it makes you laugh, especially if it makes you laugh loud and long, then it is a good joke.

The relation between laughter and comedy is much harder to define. Though most comedies do elicit at least a few smiles, laughter is a test neither for nor of comedy. By common consent, both *Lysistrata* and *The Tempest* are great comedies: *Lysistrata,* given a production that is both coarse enough and intelligent enough, is wildly funny from beginning to end; properly done, *The Tempest* is only occasionally funny, though it is thoroughly enchanting. Similarly, *Tom Jones* and *The Ambassadors* are both great comic novels: *Tom Jones* keeps a responsive reader smiling, chuckling, even laughing aloud throughout its 800-odd pages, but *The Ambassadors* raises only an occasional reflective smile from even its most enthusiastic reader. *Three Sisters* has struck any number of its viewers and readers as a sad and even gloomy play, yet it is a comedy, and a very great one, too. Even emphatically funny comedies cannot be judged in terms of the quantity of laughter they generate; on a laugh-meter *The Navigator* will outscore *The General,* yet I would not hesitate to rank *The General* as Buster Keaton's best work.

Nonetheless, all comedies, even *The Ambassadors* and *Three Sisters,* or any other works that anyone would care to describe as distinctly unfunny comedies, have something to do with laughter. We acknowledge the connection in common discourse where *comic* is a synonym for *funny* and *comedian* is a name for a person who is good at making us laugh, but we have no generally accepted theory explaining the connection. I think some theoretical explanations are possible: one would stress that comedy both values and generates gaiety, the spirit that underlies much laughter; another, much more speculative one, is that something like a joke lies at the root of every comedy. I will return to these ideas later; for now I will simply insist that an adequate theory of laughter is essential to an understanding of comedy.

Laughter is a complicated physiological, psychological, intellectual, and social phenomenon. It takes a wide variety of forms, ranging from a barely discernible upward twitch at the corners of the lips to a full, racking convulsion of the face and body. It has an even wider variety of tones, ranging from a bitter acceptance of a painful inevitability to a roaring celebration of an unexpected triumph; it can be either cold or hot and either intellectual or empty-headed. It can be oddly connected with its supposed opposite reaction, crying, for sometimes we smile through our tears and other times laugh until we cry. It can be triggered by an astonishing variety of causes—tickling, embarrassment, slips of the tongue, artful anecdotes, sheer physical or psychological exuberance—yet the effectiveness of any one of those causes is unpredictable. What makes us laugh one day leaves us stone-faced the next; what convulses one person with laughter does not cause a tremor in another.

Any attempt to proceed toward understanding by cataloging and classifying the varieties of laughter is bound to fail; the varieties and their gradations are inexhaustible. Any theory of laughter that does not take into account all of its dimensions—physiological, psychological, intellectual, or social—is also bound to fail. The best known, most frequently cited theories are those developed by Henri Bergson in *Laughter* (1900) and Sigmund Freud in *Jokes and Their Relation to the Unconscious* (1905). Bergson's central idea that we laugh at the perception of "something mechanical encrusted upon the living" is elegant and provocative, but far from comprehensive: Bergson himself is so intent on developing an argument for the social utility of laughter as a means of correcting error that he simply ignores its other dimensions. Freud's theory is harder to summarize and much harder to dismiss, but, as Freud well knew, it neither fully explains the phenomenon of laughter nor accounts for all of its causes. Two of Freud's insights are essential: that joke-work is like dream-work and that many jokes serve the purpose, often well-hidden, of venting aggression. Building on these insights of Freud and adding many of his own, Arthur Koestler developed a comprehensive theory of jokes and laughter that I think is worthy of general acceptance. Koestler first broached it in *Insight and Outlook* (1948), stated it fully in *The Act of Creation* (1964), summarized it neatly in the fifteenth edition of the *Encyclopaedia Britannica* (1974), and restated it in *Janus: A Summing Up* (1978). (All of my citations will refer to *The Act of Creation*.)

To begin with, Koestler sees laughter as a reflex—that is, as a system of partly automatic, not wholly voluntary physiological responses to a range of mental and/or physical stimuli. Though it can be faked or largely suppressed, laughter remains a reflex. But it is different from other motor reflexes, such as the contraction of the pupil of the eye in bright light, in that it does not have any apparent biological utility and may be evoked by highly complex communications as well as by simple physical stimuli.

To account for these differences, Koestler turns to Freud and argues that there is always an element of aggression or self-assertion involved in situations that provoke laughter, whether it be the mock-aggression of a mother tickling her baby or the genuine self-assertiveness of school children roaring with delight over a teacher's embarrassing slip of the tongue. Self-assertive or aggressive emotions—such as anger, lust, and fear—cause us to prepare to strike out at the world in some way or to break through the barriers of our own inhibitions; they work by triggering the adrenal glands, which in turn set off powerful and complex physiological reactions. In a primitive world or in truly dangerous circumstances, this lightning-quick mechanism is essential for survival; we must have developed it many eons ago. But in a civilized world and in peaceful circumstances, it is essential that we control this mechanism. The emotions with their capacity for adrenal stimulation will always be with us, but we cannot afford to work off their physiological consequences in "natural" ways. So, at least some of the time, we laugh instead of fighting or fleeing. To state the matter more carefully, Koestler argues that the

function of the laughter-reflex is to dissipate harmlessly the physiological reactions touched off by self-assertive or aggressive emotions when those reactions are no longer safe, desirable, or sensible.
Laughter, whether it comes as a smile or a belly laugh, whether it is
provoked by a tickling finger or a rhymed couplet, is a means of
releasing pointless tension. This squares with the common experience of man: laughter is a necessity as well as a pleasure.

The situations that produce laughter can best be described as
jokes, whether they arise accidentally in the course of life or are
contrived by man and whether they involve images, gestures, or
words. A fierce expression on the face of a puppy or a caricature of a
politician, a banana peel underfoot or a custard pie in the face, a
verbal blunder or a clever pun—all are jokes. The difficult question
is: What is a joke? Koestler answers that a joke is an arrangement
that brings about a sudden alteration in perception so that we bisociate two apparently incompatible matrices of thought with the result
that the energies aroused by the self-assertive emotions involved in
the first matrix are released to be dissipated in laughter.

Koestler speaks of a *matrix* rather than a *line* of thought because
he recognizes that thinking is not nearly so neat, so pointed, so controlled an activity as our conventional descriptions make it seem. It is
more planar than linear and involves a field of perceptions and assumptions rather than a hierarchy or subordinated set of axioms and
hypotheses. The rules of logic are more useful for analyzing and
testing the consequences of thinking than for describing its processes. At any moment during the course of thinking, the thinker is
likely to be aware of this, that, or the other thing, bringing to the
center of attention matters that had been at the periphery of concern.
However, these shifts do not take place haphazardly; there is a code,
a set of rules, governing permissible moves within a matrix of
thought. The thinker knows the code, though mostly he is not aware
of knowing it any more than a person riding a bicycle is conscious of
the code of movements that governs bicycle riding. The bike rider
does not think of what he must do to turn a corner; he just turns it.

A THEORY OF JOKES

Similarly, the thinker just shifts his attention to another matter in the field of matters relevant to the problem he is trying to solve.

Chess provides an even better analogy. The expert chess player simply knows how the pieces may move; his attention is entirely devoted to choosing from the permissible moves, the move—more accurately, the sequence of moves—that will put him in a commanding position on the board. "All coherent thinking," Koestler says, "is equivalent to playing a game according to a set of rules" (p. 39). Thinking is a marvelous, difficult, exhausting, delightful game; those who are best at it do it with playful, rather than laborious, seriousness. In this situation, matrix, which refers both to the moves that are possible and to the code of rules governing them, is the best and most comprehensively accurate term available.

When a person is doing disciplined thinking, he stays purposefully within a single matrix; when he is dreaming or daydreaming, he drifts from one matrix to another. But reality and language being what they are, a person will occasionally manage to find himself in a situation in which two matrices are simultaneously available to him, and then something very important happens—he discovers something. Much of the time his discovery turns out to be useless nonsense, but some of the time it turns out to be something of value. The nature of the "discovery" depends on a number of variables, which we need not go into here. Roughly speaking, if the person is a sage (a scientist, a philosopher, a critic, and so forth) it will be a new idea; if he is an artist, it will be a new image or metaphor; but if he is a jester (and Koestler makes it plain that we all are, or can at times be, jesters), the discovery is a new joke. Here, then, is another important value of Koestler's discussion: it lets us see that the capacity to make, or discover, jokes is a manifestation of creativity. The creative act takes many forms: joking is one of them.

The moment when two matrices are simultaneously accessible to a thinker may be most simply illustrated with a pun. Koestler offers a story from the turn of the century of "a dashing but penniless young Austrian officer who tried to obtain the favors of a fashionable courtesan. To shake off this unwanted suitor, she explained to him that her heart was, alas, no longer free. He replied politely: 'Mademoiselle, I never aimed as high as that' " (p. 36). *High,* as Koestler gently explains, has both metaphorical and topographical significance. Two ways of thinking about the courtesan, two matrices, have come together; they have "bisociated," and we can have the pleasure of thinking both ways at once. But note that there is a third matrix for *high* in this simple anecdote, an economic one: the courtesan's heart is not "free," but the penniless officer had never thought of trying to go so "high." The officer's witty reply brought together a number of understandings and made them all available at once: that the courtesan is absurdly pretentious about her essentially coarse way of life; that the officer realizes that poor young men have no business thinking of keeping mistresses; that it takes much money to maintain a fashionable, romantic attitude toward illicit sexual affairs; that it is ridiculous to talk of sexuality as a concern of the "heart"; and that a man who still has his way to make in the world is a fool if he forgets these facts, and a worse fool if he lets himself be taken in by the euphemisms and evasions of polite society. The very complexity of the pun starts to evoke complex characters in a complex social situation. It is easy to see how, for an appropriately gifted and experienced artist such as a Schnitzler or a Colette, this anecdote might serve as the germ for a piece of drama or fiction.

The anecdote also helps to explain why Koestler had to coin the term *bisociate*. *High* does not constitute a single, stable point where comparisons can be made or two straight lines of thought cross; rather, it is an area, a meeting place for several possibilities, each of which lies on and gives access to a different plane or matrix of thought. Indeed, it is a convenient simplification to term it only a *bi*sociation. No metaphor is quite adequate to the situation. However, it is pleasant, and perhaps helpful, to think of *high,* or of the key term of any good joke, as being more like a plaza where many roads merge and cross than like a street corner—specifically, as like that plaza in London where during the climactic chase in *The Lav-*

ender Hill Mob police cars coming from all points of the compass collide in one gloriously noisy heap while Alec Guinness makes his escape.

I will not take the space here to establish the validity of Koestler's theory that the central event in a joke, whether it is the product of circumstances or of human effort, is the bisociation of matrices of thought; I simply refer the skeptical to the first four chapters of *The Act of Creation*. I find Koestler's argument persuasive and useful. That is, I now find it obvious that most jokes I know involve a bisociation of matrices—for example, the recently reported piece of graffiti in a New York subway station, "If Jesus was a Jew, how come they gave him a Puerto Rican name?" Further, it gives a better—more comprehensive, less distorting, more illuminating—way of analyzing classic and "troublesome" (for analysts) jokes than other theories do. For example, Charlie Chaplin's numerous pantomime routines in which he combined the appearance of drunkenness or awkwardness with the actuality of ballet-like grace and control. Or Mark Twain's appreciation of "the calm confidence of a Christian with four aces." Or Rosalind's comment on Celia and Oliver in *As You Like It:* "They are in the very wrath of love, and they will together; clubs cannot part them."

An important advantage of Koestler's theory is that it gives a clear way of accounting for some of the glaring but often confusing truths about jokes and those who make and respond to them. Before going into that, though, I should say a little more than I already have about the role emotion plays in determining whether the event or narrative elicits "the right kind of emotional tension." The right kind can involve a number of emotions in subtle and varied mixtures, but there is always "an impulse, however faint, of aggression or apprehension." In burlesque or knockabout farce, in "sick" humor, and in most of the humor of children, the "aggressive-defensive or self-asserting tendency" is so strong that it excludes practically all other emotions. One actor bends over to pick something up and the other actor whacks him across the butt with a slapstick. " 'Why don't they let Polaks bathe in Lake Michigan?' 'Because they leave a ring.' "

And when the great Russian violinist David Oistrakh snapped a string while playing Schubert at a children's concert in Edinburgh, a thousand children who had been brought, or dragged, to the concert roared with laughter at Oistrakh's look of dismay. In more subtle, sophisticated, "adult" humor, the "aggressive-defensive or self-asserting tendency" may be nearly indiscernible, yet it is there and it is vital. "When did you begin to fall in love with Mr. Darcy?" Jane asks Elizabeth Bennet. The question is too intrusive; Elizabeth turns it away with an answer that is a counterattack on sentimental ideas of love: "When I first saw his beautiful grounds at Pemberley." Or consider the burlesque of murderous envy in the comment of Mr. Ealer in "Old Times on the Mississippi" on the pilot who had taken the boat through a tricky crossing while sleepwalking: "If he can do such gold-leaf, kid-glove, diamond-breastpin piloting when he is sound asleep, what *couldn't* he do if he were dead." Or note the beautiful fencing with the possibility of shameful exposure in Don Quixote's whispered proposition to Sancho Panza that he would agree to believe Sancho's story of what he saw while riding Clavileño's horse if Sancho would agree to believe his story of what he saw while in the cave of Montesino.

Except for the story of Oistrakh's broken string, the examples above are mine, but the argument is Koestler's. Each of the examples arouses in some degree—for persons who find them funny at all—a desire or fear that is deeply associated with the sense of self and that therefore automatically triggers the physiological reactions that are necessary for the individual human being to defend or assert himself. That inner tension we feel at the possibility of triumph or of humiliation is a gift that we have, whether we want it or not, from our most remote ancestors, and jokes play with it. Jokes set these strong reactions in motion and then suddenly reveal that there is no need for them this time. Thus, laughter is a reflex that enables the body to puff away the consequences of emotions that have been deserted, so to speak, by thought.

One of the glaring truths about jokes that Koestler's theory lets us deal with is that jokes arouse emotional responses and therefore the

A THEORY OF JOKES

emotional set of the auditor is a crucial factor in determining the nature of his response to a joke. Horace Walpole, who was struck with the role of rationality in humor, offered the formula that life is a comedy to the man who thinks and a tragedy to the man who feels. Many people have accepted this formula as a truism. Actually, it is more like a falsism, or would be if there were any such thing. A truly cold person does not laugh at all, and the satisfactions of laughter are at least as much emotional as intellectual. Thomas Hobbes was closer to truth than Walpole with his comment that "the passion of laughter is nothing else but sudden glory arising from a sudden conception of some eminency in ourselves by comparison with the infirmity of others, or with our own formerly." Unquestionably there is a Hobbesian kind of laughter, the crow of triumph; but there are a lot of other kinds, too—Quixotic, Shakespearean, Chaplinesque kinds which involve complex emotions that lie well outside the Hobbesian formula.

Koestler recognizes that though the aggressive-defensive or self-assertive emotions figure in all jokes there is ample room for other emotions, too. Those adrenaline-releasing emotions are necessary to trigger the laughter, but any given joke can—and many do—arouse other emotions as well. Guided by Koestler, one can acknowledge that love and affection as well as aggression thrive in the slapstick comedies of Laurel and Hardy, and one need not be surprised by Gulley Jimson's assertion at the end of *The Horse's Mouth* that laughing and praying are "the same thing."

The other glaring truths that Koestler's theory helps us to deal with are these: (1) that jokes and laughter require exercise of the rational faculties, yet the effect of most jokes is to affirm apparently irrational orders; (2) that while everyone talks of the importance of originality in joking, the most popular as well as the most numerous jokes are variations, often quite slight, of well-known, traditional themes; and (3) that there is no such thing as a universally funny joke; that even within a small and apparently homogeneous group, there is likely to be a wide range of responses to a given joke.

The role of rationality in joking is certainly glaring. A joke that we do not like is "stupid" and so is a person who does not "get" a joke we do like. You have to "pay attention" to a joke, and a joke, like an argument, has a "point." Jokes that are extended over several sentences are likely to have syllogistic structures and good, professional joke-makers are likely to have a strong sense of logic. Yet the more strongly a person supports an order of things that he perceives as rational, the more likely he is to view a joker as subversive. All this makes sense. Plainly, both the joker and his audience must have sufficient intellect to know one matrix of thought from another; plainly, the better they know the rules of the game governing a matrix, the more subtle and varied can be their delight in playing with those rules; and plainly, if the climax of a joke involves a sudden and therefore illogical bisociation of matrices of thought, jokes will seem to support irrationalities.

Our fondness for familiarity in jokes is also glaring, though Koestler himself chooses not to explore it. His interest is in the creative act; consequently, what he emphasizes is the way a joke can cut through layers of stale assumptions to reveal a fresh truth. Thus, for him, as for most critics, originality is the prime value in a joke, and an element of surprise is a necessity in all jokes.

Yet as all practicing comedians know, people want familiarity, not radical originality, in their jokes, and it is not so much that they want to be surprised by the climactic line of the joke as that they want to be able to pretend to be surprised by it. Steve Allen, who is himself a skillful comedian, made that clear in *The Funny Men,* a book he wrote in 1956 about the then-reigning comedians on television. He envied Jack Benny, Eddie Cantor, and certain other well-established performers because their audiences were so familiar with their material; he argued that audiences were *conditioned* to laugh at them and at their traditional gags. He cited as example a cheapskate joke from one of Jack Benny's radio programs. Everybody in the studio audience knew that Benny played the part of one of the world's stingiest men; they expected to get at least one joke about his stinginess in every skit. In this one, Benny leaves his house to walk to a neighbor's. After quite a long period of nothing but walking sounds, a notably tough voice is heard to say, "Stick 'em up. Your money or your life." A very long pause follows. Finally, the stick-up man grunts, "Come on!" and Benny replies in that querulous tone of his, "I'm thinking! I'm thinking!" On paper that does not look particularly funny, but it produced what is commonly considered to be one of the biggest laughs in the history of radio humor. There is practically nothing original in that gag; certainly, there is nothing to surprise anyone who ever heard Jack Benny do one of his skits. In fact, one of the functions of the long pause before Benny's response is to give the audience plenty of time to realize approximately what it will be. Yet the joke produced explosive laughter, even when Benny simply recounted it one night on a television talk show.

A Koestlerian analysis is easy. The matrices of money-value and of self-preservation bisociate when someone treats the traditional threat of highway robbers, "Your money or your life," as alternatives requiring serious consideration. The possibility of robbery or murder is a cue for adrenal emotions that will work on anyone not under general anesthesia. A laugh will follow when the emotion is deserted by thought. That is, laughter will follow if the audience knows that it is supposed to laugh and if the comedian has Jack Benny's polished skill in delivering a line and his absolutely perfect sense of timing.

The familiarity of the joke is crucial. The matrices that it asks people to work in are matrices that all of us have known very well for a long time; it is impossible to get lost within either, though normally we dread having to relate the two. Knowing the matrices well and knowing that Jack Benny will always make jokes about his own stinginess, we can use that long pause to try to anticipate what the climactic line will be, or to put it another way, we can build a high level of comic tension. In short, the joke gives us a role to play that we can play easily and well—we have to *pretend* to feel emotional tension and *pretend* to be surprised—and the delivery of the joke gives us plenty of time to appreciate both our own skill at pretending and Jack Benny's skill as a comedian.

Steve Allen's implication is that the most difficult problem confronting a professional comedian is to give an audience just the right amount of originality and surprise and to do it with precisely the right timing. Mistakes with respect to originality are damaging; mistakes with regard to timing are fatal.

The other glaring truth that Koestler's theory clearly explains is the one that people have the most difficulty remembering: that there is no such thing as a joke that will strike everybody as funny. When you are happily savoring the flow of wit in a Jane Austen novel or are doubled up in laughter at a W. C. Fields movie, it is impossible to believe that anyone could remain untouched by such marvelous material, yet Mark Twain proclaimed that he would not read an Austen novel for pay and many of the country's most distinguished reviewers sat stone-faced through Fields's *The Bank Dick*. This is a special problem for analysts of humor. The poor fellows cite jokes that they *know* are classics and build their analyses upon them; then reviewers take one look at their books and throw them away because the jokes are not funny.

When you look at the matter from a Koestlerian point of view, the wonder is that any jokes reach a large audience. If a given person lacks either the experience or the intellectual capacity to deal with the matrices of thought involved, he will not laugh. Or if he has had too much experience with the matrices and the way of bisociating them, he will not laugh. If for any reason he cannot even pretend to feel the requisite emotional tension, and the things that affect emotional states are legion, he will not laugh. Or if the material arouses emotions he feels he must repress, he will not laugh. If he is tone-deaf to words and inflections, if he cannot understand a gesture, if he lacks a sense of timing, if the joke offends his values or his taste, and so forth, he will not laugh.

The making of jokes is as mysterious as any other kind of creative thinking. The original joker, like the creative scientist and like the lyric poet, does not know exactly what happens at the crucial point in his work. The joke "comes to him," so swiftly sometimes that he may hear it coming out of his mouth before he realizes that he has it in his head—he may even feel like an innocent bystander who bears no responsibility for the joke. Less innocently, and more professionally, he may have been fiddling with a subject out of a hunch that a joke is there, or out of a necessity to find one, and he will have a strong, clear idea of the forms jokes can take; but he cannot deliberately manufacture the joke. Of course, if he is a skillful professional he can dust off and refurbish an old joke—indeed, that is what professionals do most of the time—but he cannot make a fresh, new joke to order. He can put up a lot of lightning rods, but he cannot command the lightning.

If the joker cannot know how the joke is made, the analyst certainly cannot describe the process in any straightforward, unambiguous way; he can only find analogies and attempt to circumscribe them with terms that are deeply metaphorical. The most fruitful and most persuasive analogy is Freud's: the making of jokes is like the making of dreams; joke-work is like dream-work. And Freud gives the best one-sentence description of the process: "a preconscious thought is given over for a moment to unconscious revision and the outcome of this is at once grasped by conscious perception" (*Jokes and Their Relation to the Unconscious,* p. 166). Like dream-work, joke-work makes heavy use of the techniques of "condensation, displacement, and indirect representation." Like dreams, jokes build on thoughts or images that the joke-maker has had more or less in awareness for some period of time. And like dreams, jokes have the characteristic of being notions that occur involuntarily. "What happens," Freud says, "is not that we know a moment beforehand what joke we are going to make, and that all it then needs is to be clothed in words. We have an indefinable feeling, rather, which I can best compare with an *absence* [the French term], a sudden release of intellectual tension, and then all at once the joke is there—as a rule ready-clothed in words" (p. 167). The dreamer is asleep, the joke-maker is awake, and joke-making is a much more rapid process. But the similarities between dreaming and joking are deep and essential.

Koestler accepts and builds on Freud's theory; indeed, he extends it to a theory of the creative act in all its forms. In the course of describing scientific creativity he emphasizes the importance of "ripeness" in creativity. A scientific discovery is made when a scientist fuses together heretofore unrelated matrices, as when Archimedes related the rise of the level of the water when he climbed into his bath to the problem of determining the volume of Hiero's crown, or when Gutenberg took part in a wine harvest and suddenly realized that if a press could squeeze the juice from grapes it could imprint letters on a page. Archimedes and Gutenberg had been trying to solve their problems for some time, but the conventional ways of thinking, the customary matrices of thought, were "blocked" and would not yield a solution. They had to put their problems to one side for a while; they had to let their minds play on the fringes of the problems. (Koestler calls this "thinking aside" and argues that it is an essential part of the creative process.) Then, at the moment of ripeness, they could achieve the seemingly irrational insights that yielded solutions; ironically, but characteristically, the discoveries then seemed obvious.

This necessity for "ripeness" explains the common phenomenon of independent simultaneous discovery of new scientific truths. It also explains why artists have "dry spells" in which they poke almost aimlessly at their work and why scholars have earned a reputation for absentmindedness. And it also helps to explain why the best jokes are usually made by people who have long had a deep need for things to laugh at. In the twentieth century the groups that have been "blocked" by prejudice—first the Irish Catholics, then the Jews, and now the Blacks—have supplied a disproportionately large number of America's best jesters.

But the fundamental block to creativity of all sorts is habit, especially a habit of thought that is condensed into a code that functions below the level of awareness and governs a way of thinking. "Habits are the indispensable core of stability and ordered behavior; they also have a tendency to become mechanized and to reduce man to the status of a conditioned automaton. The creative act, by connecting previously unrelated dimensions of experience, enables him to attain a higher level of mental evolution. It is an act of liberation—the defeat of habit by originality" (p. 96). Koestler, following

Freud, stresses that the victory is won outside the conscious mind: "The temporary relinquishing of conscious controls liberates the mind from certain constraints which are necessary to maintain the disciplined routines of thoughts but may become an impediment to the creative leap; at the same time other types of ideation on primitive levels of organization are brought into activity" (p. 169).

As so often happens, one returns to a statement of Emerson's with renewed understanding and appreciation: "The poets are free and the poets make free." The sages and the jokers are also free and also make free.

Accepting Koestler's theories of laughter and of joking makes possible some reasonably sound and helpful speculations on the troublesome matters of the relation between jokes and humor and between jokes and comedy.

The relation between jokes and humor is fairly easy to deal with. Humor presents itself as an attempt to elaborate a joke or a series of jokes by putting the joke or jokes into a context that will result in longer and louder laughter. Humor appears in literature almost always in short forms—the familiar essay, the short story, or the lyric poem. Longer works of humor usually turn out to be a series of loosely connected sketches, so loosely connected that they can be and often are printed as independent pieces. Clear examples abound in the works of the major American humorists, Mark Twain, Ring Lardner, E. B. White, S. J. Perelman, and the others.

Humor accepts the test of laughter. If it does not make you laugh or smile it has failed. Yet laughter is not its only goal, perhaps not even its main one, for humor is greatly concerned with the meanings uncovered by its jokes. Certainly jokes are meaningful, all jokes. That bisociation of matrices of thought which makes us laugh also makes us think. Humorists shape their work as much to stress the meanings as to heighten the laughter; Mark Twain said that he set out to deliver sermons and let the laughs come in as they will. Most of the best humorists are people with strong opinions, and many, like Twain or like Perelman (who emigrated to England when he became disgusted with the way things were going in this country), are notoriously testy about their opinions. As a rule, it is only the early work of the great humorists that strikes one as empty-headed; when their later work goes bad, it does so mostly because the rage generated by their meanings smothers the possibilities for laughter. In short, then, humor is more strongly duplicitous than joking. Good pieces of humor are rarer than good jokes because that strong duplicity is difficult to achieve, and it is exceedingly difficult to maintain over a long career.

Comedy's relation to jokes is far more subtle and elusive. We all feel that there is a relation, but what is it? How can we describe it? How can we relate works as complex and as varied as *Lysistrata, Don Quixote, As You Like It, Tartuffe, Pride and Prejudice, Huckleberry Finn,* and *Ulysses* to something as coarse and as commonplace and as simple (apparently) as a joke? We cannot, at least not in any firm, comprehensive way. Yet I think that Koestler makes it possible to find some truthful ways of thinking about the relation.

One must begin by assuming that comedy is fundamentally different from both tragedy and melodrama and that the difference begins with the very first perception from which the work of art grows. One can then assume that the tragic artist perceives a truth that is inescapably agonizing, that the melodramatic artist perceives a truth that is bristling with the certainty of conflict, and that the comic artist perceives a truth that is very much like a joke. I stop short of asserting that comedies begin in jokes not only because I do not know any better than anyone else does how a work of art comes into being, but also because I wish to save myself from the temptation of analyzing and classifying comedies in terms of their germinal jokes.

Yet a tentative assumption that comedies begin in jokes makes some sense. Jokes by their nature are never really simple. They always involve at least two matrices of thought—that is, two ideas plus the notions and feelings normally associated with them plus the codes (the rules of the thinking game) governing them. The more fully we respond to a joke, or perhaps I should say the more fully we lay ourselves open to it, the more strongly we will be aware of the large number of feelings, attitudes, ideas, and experiences that lie behind or beyond it. These I would term the images that arise from the joke. They are something distinct from, though in part dependent upon, the point or the meaning of the joke. The meaning of a joke is much the same for everyone who hears or perceives it. The images arising from a given joke will vary with each person responding to it. Humor is strongly concerned with the meaning of jokes; comedy explores or develops images arising from jokes and seeks to discover their significance. Comedy does not submit to the test of laughter because it is concerned not with the immediate effects of jokes but with the images that arise from them.

Jokes, then, are marvelous things. They are perfectly commonplace and accessible to everyone. Who was the first person to discover the joy of playing peek-a-boo with a baby? And who enjoys that joke more, the baby or the graybeard peeking around the corner of the crib? Life itself arranges so many of them for us it is practically impossible to avoid discovering them; indeed, even the animals find and repeat their little jokes—at least people who have studied them sympathetically swear that they do. Yet we create jokes, too. We cannot tell exactly how we do it, though it is certain that we do and that joke-making is so closely akin to the highest, most exalted forms of creativity that it shades imperceptibly into them. Most jokes seem to be eminently forgettable; one would think that they would have the life expectancy of a mayfly. Yet Mark Twain, who was surely one of the most gifted joke-makers of all time, complained bitterly of the hoariness of the jokes he heard on the frontier and was astonished to learn that a Greek had worked out the fundamental joke of his jumping frog story two thousand years before he did. Most joke-books make dreary reading, as most jokes that one hears told in the corners at cocktail parties make dreary listening; but slightly refurbished those same jokes can delight millions and one of them may very well touch off, for an artist, a major work of art.

There is no need to pile up paradoxes. Plainly jokes are one of the fundamental components of our mental life and like all truly fundamental things have an astonishing variety of functions and uses. From here I would like to go on to consider the comic vision of life that is associated with them, as chickens are associated with eggs. As I do so, a final, important value of Arthur Koestler's theory of jokes will become evident: it merges beautifully with William Lynch's theory of comedy. Koestler was a thoroughly secular man of letters, deeply involved with scientific thought; Lynch, a Jesuit theologian; there is no evidence that either considered the work of the other in developing his theory. Yet each theory confirms the other, so strongly that I can only conclude that these two very different men caught sight of the same complex truth.

2.
A
THEORY
OF
COMEDY

William Lynch develops his general theory of comedy in the first four chapters of *Christ and Apollo: The Dimensions of the Literary Imagination* (1960); I believe it is the soundest, most helpful theory available to us. It encompasses, in its own distinctive way, the understanding of the significance of comedy expressed by philosophical and anthropological critics, yet it speaks, as their theories commonly do not, to the condition of specific and diverse works of art.

Lynch's theory of comedy does not possess the magisterial power of Aristotle's theory of tragedy; no theory of comedy can. Only Western culture, which has its roots in ancient Greece, has developed a tragic vision of man's fate, and it has been expressed in only a small number of works created in a few periods of history. But comedy is ubiquitous; all major cultures and most minor ones have developed a comic vision and expressed it in diverse works in every form known to the imagination. (Anthropologists have discovered in terribly isolated valleys and jungles a few grim tribes who do not laugh and make jokes; their ways of life are so incomprehensible to the rest of us that even the anthropologists, with all their training in relating to exotic cultures, find them baffling.) The abundance of material overwhelms the theorist; he cannot examine, let alone think about, more than a small fraction of the works of comedy. Most theorists who have been trained as literary critics have responded by drastically limiting the kinds of work they consider to be comedy; many reduce comedy to a genre and deal only with the comic drama of Western culture. Elder Olson, an Aristotelian with a fine, rigorous mind, has carried this approach to a logical extreme in *The Theory of Comedy* (1968); for Olson only five of Shakespeare's plays qualify as true comedies: *The Merry Wives of Windsor, The Comedy of Errors, Love's Labor's Lost, A Midsummer Night's Dream,* and *The Taming of the Shrew.* That may seem ridiculous, but theorists who are not primarily literary critics may become so absorbed in general ideas that they fail to discuss any works of comedy in detail. Again, an excellent work stands at the extreme: Susanne K. Langer's chapter on "the comic rhythm" in *Feeling and Form* (1953) is brilliant and stimulating in its use of ideas and materials derived from anthropology, but the closest it comes to a direct examination of a work of art is a single paragraph on Schiller's *Wilhelm Tell.*

Comedy's characteristic avoidance of direct statement of theme presents theorists with another difficulty. Critics who dive deep for significance may surface with a handful of myths or just a single myth of death and rebirth, leaving behind nearly everything that distinguishes one comedy from another; Northrup Frye in *Anatomy of Criticism* (1957) is an august example. But those who shun the depths of significance may be swept into the enumeration and classification of comic devices, the shoalest water known to criticism. In either event the general reader gets little help in dealing with the compelling mysteries of particular works of art, which is probably what he was looking for when he first turned to criticism.

Lynch's view of comedy is encompassing. He sees it as a mode of the imagination, and though he is specifically concerned with the literary imagination in *Christ and Apollo,* it is plain that he would not hesitate to accept a painting by Renoir or a composition by Duke Ellington as works in the comic mode. Lynch argues that the comic mode is the most finite, most concrete, least magical, least univocal of the modes of the literary imagination; it descends dramatically through the varieties of the concrete to reach a rock-bottom reality and there discovers that life is good. To borrow a phrase from Mark Twain, a quick statement of thesis like that casts "some light but not a glare." We had better start at the beginning.

Lynch says that "the first and basic image of the literary imagination is the definite or the finite, and not the infinite, the endless, the dream" (p. 3). This is a world of particularities, not generalities, and it is the business of the literary imagination to render for us images of the particularities. Nonetheless, even in literature there is a basic conflict between imaginations that accept and glory in the concrete and limited and imaginations that yearn for and reach out for the images of unlimited, angelic power. Lynch prefers to call this a conflict between Hebraic and gnostic imaginations, but these theological terms are meant to be helpful, not restrictive. Certainly one does not have to be Hebraic in any specifically religious, racial, or cultural sense to possess an imagination Lynch would classify as Hebraic.

Lynch celebrates such a Hebraic imagination because it sees finite limitation as "the path to whatever the self is seeking: to insight, or beauty, or for that matter, to God" (p. 7). He contrasts with this idea four gnostic attitudes toward images of limitations: (1) the "magical" view, which "takes the finite as a bag of tricks, or as a set of notes to be played lightly and delicately, in order to send the soul shooting up, one knows not how, into some kind of infinite or absolute"; (2) "psychologism," which wishes "to touch the finite as lightly as possible in order to rebound, not into a quick eternity of beauty, but back into the self"; (3) the imagination of the "double vacuum," which confronts the finite only long enough to generate some emotion such as disgust and then recoils into an unsubstantial world of infinite bliss; and (4) the absurdist imagination, which holds that the finite world is indeed empty and disgusting but proudly refuses to recoil into visions of infinite, heavenly glory (pp. 8–11).

Both comedy and tragedy are modes of the Hebraic or finite imagination. In the tragic mode this imagination discovers those final moments in which human will collapses before the impossible task of measuring up to the fundamental situations of living and being: "In the end the decision of every one of the great tragedies is that, left to itself, the human will at the very height of its straining stands broken and defeated" (pp. 67–68). In the comic mode this imagination plunges as deep into the fundamental situations as it does in the tragic mode but without such awareness of pain and of striving; in doing so it destroys the categories (the rich, the proud, the mighty, and so forth) within which most of life is spent and thereby discovers—or decides—that being is "profoundly and funnily unbreakable [and] has no needs above itself" (p. 91).

Lynch's understanding of the relation between tragedy and comedy is similar to Frye's in that both see comedy as including but moving beyond the materials of tragedy. In *Anatomy of Criticism* Frye states his understanding in Jungian terms, holding that tragedy deals with only part of the cycle of myth while comedy deals with the full cycle. Lynch, who cannot accept Jungian psychology, as he explains in *Images of Faith* (1973), states his understanding in terms of a plunge into the finite. Tragedy plunges in to leave us fully cognizant of the abyss between the power of our wills and the actuality of our needs; comedy plunges in to discover that when we wholly submit to it the finite itself generates the insight we need.

Perhaps the plainest illustration of his concept of the generative finite is the aging process. The best way to understand, or at least to dissipate, the confusions of one age is to proceed into the ages that follow. Nothing relieves the miseries of adolescence like living through maturity into middle age, and it is not possible to sustain the sense of crisis that afflicts so many of us in middle age through old age. The one sure cure for old age is, of course, death. (The terrible thing about our "image industries"—Lynch's useful term for the purveyors of dreams for the masses—is their hostility to the processes of aging; they want to fix all of us in our years of furious consumption, the devil take the psychic consequences.) Even within a single stage of life or a limited area of experience, Lynch would argue, the finite generates understanding and acceptance. Thus, doctors have recently been demonstrating that dying itself is an instructive process and that most people passing through it in anything like full awareness come to a calm acceptance of their own deaths. The same is true for grief; it is a curative process and those who are narcotized through its early stages emerge less strong than those who confront it fully.

For further, and quite different, illustrations of the idea of the generative finite one could turn to any of the numerous scenes in literature in which a comic hero works his way out of difficulties by plunging deeper into them. *Huckleberry Finn* is practically one long illustration, reaching its climax when Huck resolves his problems as a social outcast by deciding, "All right, then, I'll *go* to hell."

A THEORY OF COMEDY

The notion of trusting finite experience of all sorts to lead us through to understanding of the problems and confusions we discover in it is disturbing, even threatening, to a certain kind of mind that prides itself on its logical capacities. Lynch calls it the univocal mind, and he argues that comedy most certainly is hostile to it. It is "that kind of mind which, having won through to all the legitimate unities and orderings of the logical and rational intelligence, insists, thereafter, on descending through the diversities, densities, and maelstroms of reality in such a way as to give absolute shape to it through these unities and orderings" (p. 107). To put it informally, the univocal mind is so pleased with its ability to abstract generalizations from the welter of experience that it cannot bear to think of things as anything but examples of the generalizations which it has mastered. It is a mind that having discovered the concept of stimulus and response can reduce psychology to behaviorism, or that having inherited the concept of the market can persist in describing a modern economy as though it were a hotbed of competition, or that having fastened onto the concept of myth can treat literature as nothing but the art of refurbishing ancient legends. For a single, appallingly sufficient illustration of that mind at work consider American policy in Vietnam, 1965–1975.

To the univocal mind with its insistence on deriving abstractions and on projecting them back on reality Lynch contrasts the analogical mind which delights in discovering similarities and pursuing them through the diversity that reality offers. It is a mind that can observe a set, think accurately about whatever it is that the members of the set have in common, and relish the qualities that distinguish one member of the set from another. To give a simple example, the analogical mind can observe a set of university faculty, deal effectively with the interests their status as faculty members binds them to, and never make the mistake of treating any group of them as interchangeable units, or any one of them as simply or even primarily as a professor in a university. It is not necessary to follow Lynch's discussion of analogical thinking through a summary of Plato's ideas in the *Parmenides* and on into the theological issues that are the main concern of the latter part of *Christ and Apollo;* for my purposes here it is enough to recognize that he gives us a very clear way of understanding that comedy is not anti-intellectual, it is merely anti-univocal. Note how well this fits with Koestler's theory of jokes: the bisociation of matrices will probably delight an analogical mind while it may leave a univocal mind uneasy and suspicious of the jester's motives; or to reverse the emphasis, the analogical mind is far more likely than the univocal mind to search for and discover places where matrices of thought may bisociate.

One more implication in Lynch's theory must be stressed before I can discuss the recurrence of certain major images in comedy: the function of comedy is to sustain hope. Lynch first broaches this idea in his discussion of the power of the Hebraic imagination's acceptance of images of limitation: "In taking this narrow path [of the finite] directly, we shall be using our remembered experience of things seen and earned in a cumulative way, to create hope in the things that are not yet seen" (p. 7). He returns to it in his chapter on tragedy where he argues that there are three different levels on which life can be lived. The first is "the level of surfaces and superficiality" on which technological nations too often try to live. Beneath that is the much deeper level where pain and chaos are indeed confronted; this is the level of those who take pride and grim pleasure in "facing the facts." But deeper still is the level on which human pride and will and capacity arrive at real helplessness; this is the tragic level of existence. Yet comedy, too, explores this third level, for this is the place of hope. "The principal message of the theologian about hope is that it is the meeting ground of the tragic awareness of helplessness in the human will and its taking up (in the same moment) the strength of God" (p. 79). In the chapter on comedy Lynch avoids using the term *hope;* rather, he describes that "rock-bottom reality in man" which comedy discovers as "the most inherently confident rung of the finite. It is ugly and strong" (p. 91).

Any emphasis on the hopefulness of comedy is likely to embarrass serious modern readers almost as much as emphasis on comic ribaldry embarrassed our Victorian predecessors, perhaps because we have invested so much effort and pride in "facing the facts" on that second level of existence. We would be less embarrassed by hopefulness if we did not confuse it with wishful thinking and if we could rid ourselves of the silly notion that it is better—tougher, more manly, more realistic, more courageous—to look at the bleak side of everything. The corollary of hoping is wishing, not wishful thinking. Hoping and wishing are, as Lynch stresses in *Images of Hope* (1965), positive acts, essential components of the drive to move toward the world outside oneself; from either an evolutionary or an individual perspective, they are necessities of life. Wishful thinking is nearly their exact opposite, for it is essentially a yearning that the world come to oneself, and on one's own terms. It leads directly to stagnation, apathy, and despair. There is certainly an abundance of wishful thinking behind fashionable pessimism—if the world is doomed anyway, then there is no point in changing my self at all—and even more underlies the glorification of toughness in contemporary popular culture. Actually it is hopefulness that calls for inconvenient kinds and quantities of courage; it requires first that we search what is out there to find if there is some way or place we may thrive, and then that we change, or at least abandon our pretensions, in order to fit into that place. That is why the great, hopeful comedies so consistently celebrate the virtues of courage and gaiety.

As I suggested earlier, Lynch's theory of comedy is extraordinarily helpful as one deals with the striking recurrences in comic literature—with the themes, gestures, ideas, attitudes, and relationships appearing in comedy after comedy. Lynch uses the comprehensive term *images* to refer to these things. He never speaks of the ideas or themes of comedy and only rarely of its meanings, and he is far more concerned with symbolic gestures (in language as well as in actions) than with statements.

Images is an accurate term for what comedy seeks to communicate to us. Images tend to be inclusive rather than exclusive, to be more or less well-focused rather than well-defined, to be aesthetically coherent rather than logically sound. For example, *As You Like It* does not give us any ideas about amorous love, only images of what it is like. The play has no programmatic schemes for the purveyors and consumers of "how to" books on sex and marriage, only the radiant image of a woman who is many fathoms deep in love and who will therefore cure her beloved of his fondness for writing bad, lovesick verses. Or consider "Old Times on the Mississippi," which is so free of ideas that a critic must struggle to find anything to explicate in it, and *Huckleberry Finn,* which carries the warning that anyone searching for ideas in it will be shot by order of the author. Yet the images that Mark Twain gave us in these works are deeply, unforgettably significant.

Image may well be the correct term for any complex understanding, despite the way it has been degraded by advertising salesmen and political pundits. It avoids the claims to objectivity and certainty implicit in the term *knowledge* and identifies the crucial truth that an understanding is an organization of information, ideas, and values which can strengthen or weaken as an organism does. (For an extended discussion of this idea, see Kenneth Boulding, *The Image,* 1956.) It is also openly metaphorical and therefore faithful to the fact that we cannot directly describe consciousness and thought; the process of picture-making is a good mirror in which to catch a glimpse of those mental processes we cannot observe directly. Finally, *image* fits well with Koestler's term *matrix* with its stress on the planar rather than the linear quality of purposeful thought.

I identify five major recurring images in comic literature. These are comedy's images of intellect, of will, of wishfulness, of time and change, and of play. Lynch's theory of comedy responds to each of these images and leads to a fuller understanding of each and of how they relate to each other.

First, there is the matter that has struck almost everyone who has looked at the subject—comedy's odd, difficult-to-define image of the intellect. The man of intellect is a classic butt of comedy—Pangloss, for example—yet the clod and the practical man of affairs are equally classic figures of ridicule. There is no question that stupidity is a prime subject of comic derision, but there is a question whether comedy sees more of it in boneheads or in logicians. All of the great comedies make us pause on the question of the right use of or, better, the right relation with the intellect. For one fine, superbly troubling example take *The Misanthrope*. The best intellect in the play belongs to Alceste, but unquestionably Célimène, who seems to be much too playful to think, and Philinte, who seems to be a stick in the middle of the road, and even Eliante, who is just a nice girl, all possess more wisdom than Alceste. For other, possibly more surprising examples, take the plays of George Bernard Shaw, who seems always in danger of being swept away in admiration of intellect in general and his own intellect in particular. *Man and Superman* shows Ann Whitefield triumphing in mind as well as body over Jack Tanner, and *Saint Joan* celebrates the purity and power of a mind that does not have to think through ideas in order to grasp truths.

Lynch's explanation, as I have already indicated, is clear: comedy is hostile to the univocal mind. It rejects the neat, mechanical, perfectly balanced orders generated by logic and embraces the organic, irregular orders generated by what Lynch calls the analogical mind. In logic, this must follow from that; in comedy, this will probably follow from that. In logic the best circle is a perfect circle, but in comedy irregular circles are much better than perfect ones. In logic the test of a thesis is its ability to generate perfectly predictable results; in comedy the goal is to generate orders of living that are predictable in general and unpredictable in detail. To the univocal mind comedy frequently seems anarchic; but in truth comedy delights in traditions, rituals, and patterns, in returns that are similar but never identical.

Two quotations from the notebooks of Renoir speak forcefully for the analogical mind: "Don't be afraid to look at the great masters of the best periods. They created irregularity within regularity. Saint Mark's Cathedral in Venice: symmetrical, as a whole, but not one detail is like another." "I propose to found a society. It is to be called 'The Society of Irregulars.' The members would have to know that a circle should never be round" (*Renoir, My Father,* pp. 243, 245).

Lynch's theory of comedy is the most helpful that I know in understanding comedy's powerful and distinctive image of the intellect. It is equally helpful in dealing with the associated matter of comedy's image of the will.

Comedy consistently mocks willfulness, pride of purpose, and self-centered design, especially when they are associated with schemes of action that have or are likely to have public approval or when they involve a claim to godlike dignity or power. As a precise example Lynch offers the British film made in the fifties *Tight Little Island* (called *Whisky Galore* in Britain). Its subject is the events following the wreck of a ship carrying a full load of Scotch whisky on an island in the Hebrides; the time is World War II and the islanders have consumed their full ration of whisky. The film celebrates, exuberantly, the resourcefulness of the islanders in getting the whisky off the wreck and in hiding it; at the same time it mocks, remorselessly, the man of authority who is determined to enforce the customs laws and who boasts that when he starts a thing he pushes it all the way through.

The extent of comedy's attack on willfulness can be seen by considering the nature of the conventional butts of ridicule in farce—the miser, the lustful or jealous old man, the pompous master, the scheming woman, and so forth—or by selecting any group of comedies on military life and seeing what happens to the purposeful, vigorous, prideful heroes and leaders—for example, the colonels and generals in *Catch-22*. Perhaps the most precise example is Lady Catherine in *Pride and Prejudice* as she makes known her resolve that Elizabeth shall not marry Darcy, but for variety and subtlety in sustained mockery of fatheaded willfulness it is hard to improve on the plays of Molière.

Comedy's heroes are not men of action who can impose their will upon circumstances; at most, they are men and women, frequently somewhat the worse for wear, who have the wit to keep circumstances from imposing on them, such as Dorine in Molière's *Tartuffe*, Egbert Sousé in W. C. Fields's *The Bank Dick*, or Jim Dixon in Kingsley Amis's *Lucky Jim*. Most characteristically, they seem to be conspicuously lacking in heroic qualities: they are women (Lysistrata or Viola), or dreamers (Parson Adams), or outcasts

(Huck and Jim), or shabby artists (Gulley Jimson), or even boobs (Laurel and Hardy). Shaw made this point in *Arms and the Man* when he contrasted the dashing, conventional hero, Sergius, with the frightened, chocolate-eating hero, Bluntschli. The slogan of the heroes of comedy might well be Yossarian's "I'm going to live forever, or die trying." Certainly their most representative gesture would be Quixote's dropping of the reins in order to let Rocinante decide which direction they should take at the beginning of his second sally.

Deep in the comic scheme of things is a preference for those who float through life over those who march through life, for those who do what "it" wants them to do and go where "it" wants them to go over those who do and go according to resolute purposes of their own. "It" may be understood in any number of ways—as God or the life force, as the Mississippi River or as the Pacific Ocean, as the spirit of the earth or as the wisdom of the senses—but always "it" is something outside the hero's mind. He has the courage, faith, and humility to submit to "it." This submission is what Whitman argues for in "Song of Myself." *Lean, loafe, drift, float, lie, dream, wait, die*—these are the key verbs for Whitman as he sounds his "barbaric yawp over the roofs of the world."

The key elements of Lynch's theory—comedy's acceptance of the finite and limited, its suspicion of all "magical" or "angelic" modes of imagining, its hostility to the univocal, abstracting intellect, and its hopefulness—make it easy to explain why a combination of mockery of willfulness and celebration of Whitmanesque passivity is a constantly recurring image in comic literature.

The third significant image that Lynch's theory permits one to deal with clearly is comedy's mockery of wishful thinking, though as I argued earlier one must carefully distinguish between wishing and wishfulness. Wishing for what is or might be is a delightful, life-sustaining act, and one of the most basic patterns in comic stories is the unexpected fulfillment of what were, after all, realistic wishes. But no one is more consistently and more harshly mocked in comedy than the person who wishfully denies the real nature of things. The point is so obvious that it needs no arguing, but for a single classic illustration think of Lady Wishfort (in *The Way of the World*) arranging herself upon the couch to receive a visit from what she much too wishfully thinks will be an ardent suitor.

A useful, alternative way of stating essentially the same point is that comedy consistently calls for double vision, for the ability to see this *and* that at the same time and to see both accurately. It takes some gift for wishing to maintain acute double vision in contradictory circumstances, which are the circumstances most of us live in. Conversely, comedy derides clods and pedants who are able to see only one thing at a time. "Who cares," sings Cummings, "if some one-eyed sonofabitch invents an instrument to measure spring with?"

Lady Wishfort is ridiculous because she sees everything in terms of her own sexual yearning; Millamant and Mirabell are admirable because they see doubly. Yes, their deepest wish is for each other, but that is no reason to throw away a fortune. True, in their private lives they are very much in love, but that is all the more reason for not making fools of themselves in their social lives. The contract scene is a lovely celebration of their powers of double vision.

Comedy is a mode for realistic, wishing but not wishful, imaginations. "It is the most cognitive and least magical of the arts" (*Christ and Apollo,* p. 96).

A fourth major image of comedy is its image of time and change as cyclical and unthreatening. Comedy's propensity for seeing time as cyclical and repetitive rather than as linear and progressive is well known and often discussed. Progressions—of seasons and of generations—matter in comedy; progress does not. Mutability and flux may disturb certain kinds of Romantic imaginations, like Shelley's, and modern imaginations that for psychic or social or religious reasons yearn for a restful point of stasis; but the comic imagination is undisturbed by mutability and at ease with flux. Though it startles many people to describe Thoreau as a comic artist, I think that *Walden* is, among other things, a particularly full exploration of the comic image of time.

For a brief, pungent rendition of this image I cite the closing scene of Synge's *The Playboy of the Western World* when old Mahon comes crawling in while Michael James and the others are trying to get Christy safely tied up:

> CHRISTY: *(Scrambling on his knees face to face with old Mahon)* Are you coming to be killed a third time, or what ails you now?
>
> MAHON: For what is it they have you tied?
>
> CHRISTY: They're taking me to the peelers to have me hanged for slaying you.
>
> MICHAEL: *(Apologetically)* It is the will of God that all should guard their little cabins from the treachery of law, and what would my daughter be doing if I was ruined or was hanged itself?
>
> MAHON: *(Grimly, loosening Christy)* It's little I care if you put a bag on her back and went picking cockles till the hour of death; but my son and myself will be going our own way, and we'll have great times from this out telling stories of the villainy of Mayo, and the fools is here. *(To Christy, who is freed)* Come on now.
>
> CHRISTY: Go with you, is it? I will then, like a gallant captain with his heathen slave. Go on now and I'll see you from this day stewing my oatmeal and washing my spuds, for I'm master of all fights from now. *(Pushing Mahon)* Go on, I'm saying.
>
> MAHON: Is it me?
>
> CHRISTY: Not a word out of you. Go on from this.
>
> MAHON: *(Walking out and looking back at Christy over his shoulder)* Glory be to God! *(With a broad smile)* I am crazy again!
>
> *(Goes.)*
>
> CHRISTY: Ten thousand blessings upon all that's here, for you've turned me a likely gaffer in the end of all, the way I'll go romancing through a romping lifetime from this hour to the dawning of the judgment day.
>
> *(He goes out.)*

Old Mahon, who thought that Christy was a milksop, has found that his son is a better man than he is, so he is happy. Christy, who thought that he was a useless fool and coward, has discovered that he really is the Playboy of the Western World, so he is happy. Change is marvelous, and time, "from this hour to the dawning of the judgment," is a spacious opportunity for romancing and romping.

Lynch devotes an entire chapter in *Christ and Apollo* to the subject of time, arguing that "there are basically two contrary and hostile positions now held by the contemporary imagination regarding time," one seeing it as a thing that must be escaped from and the other seeing it as "nothing but *ourselves,* as we move without pause through all the phases and stages of our lives" (p. 33). Comedy comes out of this latter, time-embracing imagination. In the chapter devoted especially to comedy he stresses in his discussion of various specific works "comic remembrance." He is convinced that "the one offense . . . which comedy cannot endure is that a man should forget he is a man, or should substitute a phony faith for faith in the vulgar and limited finite" (p. 97). Given these ideas of Lynch's, it is obvious that comedy from the Greeks to the present would image time and change as cyclical and unthreatening. Why should a comedian fear the law and nature of his own being?

Finally, I come to the most obvious, most basic, and yet in some ways most puzzling image of comedy. Lynch avoids naming it, even though it is the central subject of his chapter on comedy. He contents himself with a final, deceptively simple assertion: "For things *are* funny and a final theory of comedy must be as simple as that" (p. 110). I will put a label on it, if only for the sake of convenience, and call it the image of play. In doing so I have in mind not only that "free activity" which Johan Huizinga characterizes in *Homo Ludens: A Study of the Play Element in Culture* as standing "quite consciously outside 'ordinary' life as being 'not serious' " (p. 13), but also the possibility of treating even the most ordinary and serious of activities as though it were, like play, free of worldly purpose, simply the utterly absorbing occasion for fun. To put it another way, the image requires a label that is part noun, part adjective, and part verb, for it refers both to the activity, play, and the manner, playful, and also carries an injunction, play! The image is the source of that spirit of gaiety which permeates all comedy and which is the one thing that all of us are sure to carry away from any comedy we respond to; and it is grounded on the conviction that the unknown will turn out to be at least as good as the known, that we will, somehow, land right side up. Sometimes, as in black comedy and gallows humor, the conviction is heavily tinged with desperation; sometimes, in sunny, romantic comedies, it is marked by an exuberance for which there is little reasonable justification. Comedy trusts play as a way of knowing and as a way of doing—which is why it is so liable to strike respectable people as irresponsible, or even subversive. Certainly comedy prefers playful people to solemn. Ernest Hemingway spoke for everyone who has ever imagined in the comic mode when he made his comment on the playful, doomed painter Pascin: "They say seeds of what we will do are in all of us, but it always seemed to me that in those who make jokes in life the seeds are covered with better soil and with a higher grade of manure" (*A Moveable Feast*, p. 104).

Obvious as it is, comedy's image of play has been a problem for theorists of comedy and for the most part they have treated it only in passing. Frye is so concerned with mythic patterns that he largely ignores it. Bergson is so intent on arguing comedy's value as a social corrective that he responds only to the kinds of playfulness that produce useful mockery. And though George Meredith stresses the playfulness of the Comic Spirit, he is willing to give status only to refined forms of play. But Lynch's whole approach to comedy makes it easy for him to put playfulness, or funniness, at the center of the subject. An acceptance of limitations with a concomitant rejection of "magical" solutions and "angelic" powers points toward a delight in games (with all their arbitrary rules about fair and foul balls) and in unabashed pretense. Absorption in the concrete and trust in the generative finite lead directly to full, innocent acceptance of the present moment, which is the essence of play. Hostility toward the univocal and celebration of the analogical mind and imagination compel one to respect witty, playful ways of thinking. Above all, an argument that the course of comedy is a descent below all the categories to rock-bottom reality, "which is profoundly and funnily unbreakable," is an argument that comedy is a call to play, an invitation to dance.

The deepest image of comedy is its image of play, for that image is the product of its images of the intellect, of the will, of hope, and of time.

One last point about Lynch's theory remains to be discussed: his argument that one must distinguish between true comedy and false comedy. I resisted the argument for a long time, and on apparently good ground. First, I distrust negative judgments—my own, certainly, and others's, probably. Negative judgments tend to be self-protective, for the surest way of warding off bad news is to refuse to admit the messenger. Positive judgments are more reliable, if only because there is more illumination in delight than in disgust. This is especially true when the subject is comedy because comedy is connected with jokes, and responses to jokes, as Koestler makes plain, can be distorted by any number of extraneous things. If you like a joke, you can be sure that it is good, at least for you and probably for many other people. If you dislike a joke, you can only be sure that it did not work for you; the world might be full of people who would love it. Second, Lynch's distinction between true and false comedy looks like an invitation to circular reasoning. You formulate your theory on the basis of selected pieces of comedy and then denounce as false comedies that do not fit your theory. It looks like a dance around the mulberry bush.

But appearances are deceiving, in arguments as in people. The distinction is not merely valid, it is essential. You cannot begin to think accurately about comedy until you have made it. Like sex, comedy comes in true and false forms. (Needless to say, this improper analogy is mine, not Father Lynch's.) False comedy, like false sex, is radically misleading; it may be titillating, like a centerfold in *Playboy*, but it denies the essential nature of the genuine article. The essence of true comedy and true sex is that they demand a lot of their participants and reward them with a joyful confidence that looks downright foolish to outsiders.

Dropping the analogy, I appeal to common experience. We all know that there is such a thing as false laughter because we have all indulged in it. Most often, I trust, we have done so out of politeness or nervousness. Why offend relatives, acquaintances, or bosses by not laughing at what they obviously find funny? But we have all giggled for other, nastier reasons as well—to shirk the demands of our own values or to flatter ourselves with a little wishful thinking. I know that I am not the only person who has laughed at bigoted jokes in spite of my own contempt for bigotry, nor am I the only one who has gladly paid the price of a little phoney laughter for the sake of a chance to dodge a reality that I know perfectly well I should confront.

If there are such things as true and false laughter, there have to be such things as true and false jokes and true and false comedy. The only question, then, is how do we make the distinction?

Lynch does so by beginning with the idea that though there are in true comedy "different levels of comic remembrance . . . they are all somehow one in some kind of love of the human and some kind of refusal to be ashamed of human parentage" (p. 98). He argues that in pseudocomedy four forms of remembrance flourish that attempt to deny humanness; such remembrance may elicit laughter, but not the joy, acceptance, and triumphant confidence generated by true comedy. The false forms of remembrance are those of the clown, of the meticulous man, of disgust, and of hatred.

The remembrance of the clown is basically sad, full of "self-pitying spirituality," because the clown feels trapped in the human condition and invites pity for the fate he will eventually suffer. On the other hand, the meticulous man feels himself superior to the human condition, or at least to its more vulgar manifestations. In both cases, Lynch is able to cite distinguished artists as his examples: for the clown, Chaplin, and for the meticulous man, Shaw. From 1930 on, Chaplin's work was deeply flawed by self-pity, and Shaw always tended to feel entitled to handle ordinary human vulgarity with tongs.

Disgust as a false form of remembrance is harder to pin down because there is an element of something that is like disgust in a lot of true comedy. Perhaps it is best to describe it as remembrance that begins in sardonic amusement at the monstrous and ends in a marked preference for the nonhuman. Lynch cites Puck as his example of this kind of false comedian, for Puck takes delight in making poor Bottom *really* an ass. "The variety of Pucks in human history have been endless. They are never comic. In most cases they are harmless; in others their essentially nonhuman point becomes startlingly clear" (p. 105). He gives a startlingly clear example: the Romans who, like Heliogabalus, paid premium prices at the slave market for horribly deformed and idiotic children because they found them amusing.

The false remembrance of hatred arises from the exasperation that pure, univocal intelligence feels when it is confronted by the stubbornly "impure" nature of man and of his works. Wanting things to be either wholly angelic or simply gross, it directs diabolical laughter toward everything that insists on being both at once. Lynch gives as his example the laughter of Andrian Leverkuhn, the hero of Thomas Mann's *Doctor Faustus*.

Without disagreeing with Lynch's categories of false laughter, I offer another, broader way of distinguishing between true and false comedy. False comedy tends to flatter its audience; the intellectual and psychic demands that it makes are few and unthreatening. The false comedian strikes a bargain with his audience, though either or both may not permit themselves to be aware of it. The bargain is that if you will let me mock you a little and if you will admire my cleverness in mocking, I will let you admire your own cleverness in responding to the mocking and send you forth with a reinforced conviction of your own superiority to those things and those persons you wish to feel superior to. Of course, that leaves the maker feeling superior to the audience, but if he has any skill at all, he enters enough disclaimers to still that thought, and if he has great commercial gifts, he so thoroughly identifies with the audience that disclaimers are unnecessary.

True comedy is harder on everyone concerned because it insists that maker and audience alike are part of whatever is being laughed at. To accept that identification we almost always have to give up a number of psychic comforts and frequently a number of intellectual ones as well. True comedy does not so much strike bargains as make demands, though always there is the implied promise that if we will first sacrifice our complacencies, we will later gain some fundamental security.

The distinction between true and false comedy and comedians is neither simple nor sharp-edged, though it is of fundamental importance. Mostly, one cannot say quickly whether this work or that comedian is true or false, and when one has made the judgment, it is likely to be, like all critical judgments, debatable. That does not matter, because the distinction is not a magic wand for separating good from bad or great from minor; it is simply something we must do, somehow, in some terms, before we can think sensibly about the nature and significance of the comic vision. Some gifted, skillful people create comedy for commercial use; their works must be admired for their technique, yet they must finally be judged false. Some true comedians are clumsy at times and are obviously limited in the range of material they can deal with and of effects they can produce; their works may not be great, but to a discerning eye they possess distinct and solid value.

It will take extensive discussion in subsequent chapters to clarify the distinction, but a brief contrast and a single unusual example will be helpful here. For me, as for William Lynch, Chaplin is a suspect comedian. I have little trouble accepting his early work, but in time he seems to become anxious to separate himself from the comic role that he plays. In the late films the separation becomes formal: he may have to advertise them as starring Charlie Chaplin, but the screen credits solemnly inform us that Charles Chaplin wrote the music (which, incidentally, is banal) and directed and produced the film. Lynch quotes Chaplin as saying when he stopped playing the role of the tramp Charlie, "I've finally gotten rid of the little bastard." But I think the attitude appears, with damaging effect, even in films Chaplin made in the twenties. Specifically, I see it in the famous close-up that ends *City Lights*—the tramp, a flower in his hand and an index finger on his teeth, smiles in embarrassment and hope at the beautiful flower girl who has just realized that he is the "millionaire" who paid for the operation that rescued her from blindness. There is nothing wrong with that as a way to finish the movie's

Victorian plot. What bothers me is the way the lighting and the soft focus of the camera emphasize the brimming beauty of Chaplin's eyes. Here, and in many other places in his films of the twenties, Chaplin seems anxious to remind us that he is not really a tramp, that inside the costume and the role stands a beautiful man. He can and does make us laugh, but he shows us that he is not merely a comedian. The combination is comforting to those of us who fear that laughter is a sign of coarseness. But even if Lynch and I are right that "self-pitying spirituality" gives falsity to Chaplin's comedy, Chaplin remains an important, gifted film comedian; too many accomplished filmmakers have spoken eloquently of what they have found in his work for us to dismiss him.

In contrast to Chaplin I cite Buster Keaton, who was, I think, a true comedian. In his great years in the twenties, before he was ruined by a bad marriage and Metro-Goldwyn-Mayer, Keaton gave himself as fully to his comedy as he possibly could; certainly he never asked his audience to see any difference between him and the gloriously impassive "slow thinker" he portrayed. Though he was an extraordinarily handsome man he never seemed aware of the fact. Indeed, *College* loses some of its credibility, and Keaton was always concerned about keeping his farce credible, because he has to portray a clumsy student doggedly trying to make an athletic hero of himself. It works fairly well when he is wearing a football uniform, but when he appears in a track suit it is impossible to believe that a man with such a beautifully proportioned, finely muscled body could be athletically inept. A scene in *The General* gives us an exact measure of the difference between Keaton and Chaplin. Where Chaplin maneuvered the final shot in *City Lights* to reveal the beauty of his eyes, Keaton maneuvers the only shot in *The General* that concentrates on his dark, distinctively shaped eyes to create one of the funniest gags in the film. He is an engineer alone in an engine and tender on a Southern railroad during the Civil War in mad pursuit of some Northern spies because they have stolen his own beloved engine, The General. In an effort to slow his pursuit, the spies have unhitched a freight car from their train, forcing Keaton to push it before him. When he turns to get wood from the tender to throw into the firebox, the freight car is accidentally shunted onto a siding. (Never mind the details; Keaton makes it all plausible.) When he returns to the controls, the camera focuses on his eyes: they pop slightly when he realizes, a trifle late, that the freight car is no longer there; then in a gesture of marvelous, furtive idiocy they dart to the side to see if it is running alongside the engine even though there is no track there.

Keaton's face, especially when seen in profile, looked like it had been copied from some ancient Greek urn or Egyptian mural. If Keaton "used" that quality at all, he used it as part of his comedy; he did not separate the beautiful from the funny. He did not strike any comfortable bargains with his audience any more than he did with the succession of pretty girls who played the slow thinker's sweethearts. Poor Marian Mack must have acquired a lot of bruises playing Annabel Lee in *The General,* but in the world of Buster Keaton everybody must take his lumps. That is why it is such a truly funny world.

One final example comes from Henry Miller, who is, I think, a true comedian and whose works I discuss in the next chapter. It is the letter he wrote in 1959 in response to his lawyer's request for a statement that could be used in connection with the review by the Supreme Court of Norway of a decision by the Oslo Town Court that *Sexus* is an obscene work. (It is reprinted under the title "Defense of the Freedom to Read" in *Versions of Censorship,* ed. John McCormick and Mairi MacInnes.)

Miller was exasperated by the absurd, lengthy document in which the lower court explained its opinion. "If I were there, in the dock," he says, "my answer would probably be—'Guilty! Guilty on all ninety-seven counts! To the gallows!' For when I take the short, myopic view, I realize I was guilty even before I wrote the book. Guilty, in other words, because I am the way I am. The marvel is that I am walking about as a free man. I should have been condemned the moment I stepped out of my mother's womb" (p. 224). Nevertheless, Miller goes on to explain with some patience that he and his book are neither any worse nor any better than other men and other books. Refusing to get drawn into the conventional legal game of citing "authorities" who praise his work, he simply argues that proscribing his book would do no good for the members of the court, for the ideal of law, or for the people of Norway. "It is not something evil, not something poisonous, which this book *Sexus* offers the Norwegian reader. It is a dose of life which I administered to myself first, and which I not only survived but thrived on. Certainly I would not recommend it to infants, but then neither would I offer a child a bottle of *aqua vite*" (p. 230).

Miller meets the demand that true comedy makes on us all. We must begin by pleading "Guilty! Guilty on all ninety-seven counts!" Then, and probably only then, can we discover the real absurdity and futility of the charges and finally conclude—with a little luck—that the dose of life which has been administered to us is one we cannot only survive but thrive on.

3.
TRUE
COMEDIANS
AND
FALSE

William Lynch may have been the first critic to insist on the importance of distinguishing between true comedy and false, but comic artists have been making the distinction all along. What could be termed the theme of the false comedian recurs throughout comic literature.

Most often it is given only relatively brief, farcical treatment, as in the scenes of *A Connecticut Yankee in King Arthur's Court* in which The Boss resists the impulse to murder various would-be comedians in Arthurian England. Fielding does much more than that with the theme in *Joseph Andrews* through his blistering portraits of the "roasting" squire, Beau Didapper, and all of the self-important mockers in the various inns that Parson Adams and Joseph visit. James Joyce deals pungently with it in *Ulysses,* most notably in his portrait of Buck Mulligan. It is important in Vladimir Nabokov's *Lolita,* in the contrast between Clare Quilty and Humbert Humbert, and in *The Horse's Mouth,* in the contrast between Bisson, the fake artist, and Gulley Jimson. Henrik Ibsen treats the theme in his own harsh way—with what Shaw calls his "iron humor"—in the last act of *The Wild Duck* through Relling's attack on Gregers Werle's "idealism." Synge's central contrast in *The Playboy of the Western World* between Christy and his father on the one hand and the people around Pegeen Mike on the other is a contrast between true and false comedians; Christy and his father are finally free to "go romancing through a romping lifetime from this hour to the dawning of the judgment day" while the people in the shebeen, who cannot stand comic truth when it becomes actual, are left to creep through the rest of their lives in County Mayo. The theme is central in nearly all of Ring Lardner's work, for Lardner was bitterly fascinated by the inept and cruel jokers that he saw flourishing in American life. "Haircut" is the classic example, but one could also cite *You Know Me, Al,* most of the stories about professional sports and the entertainment business, and the stories in *Gullible's Travels*. Finally, there is Shakespeare, who kept returning to the theme in one form or another throughout his comedies. He does it most frequently by contrasting artful, deliberate fools—Feste, Touchstone, and Falstaff—with blundering, fatuous fools—Malvolio, Jaques, and Justice Shallow. But his portrait of Puck in *A Midsummer Night's Dream* serves Lynch as a classic type of one sort of false comedian; and if only because Ariel is in some ways kin to Puck, one can find among all the subtly interwoven themes of *The Tempest* the theme of the false comedian.

However, for close, intricate, fascinating studies of the difference between true and false comedians I turn to *Don Quixote* and *Huckleberry Finn*. Dissimilar as they are in nearly all other respects, these two authoritative comedies agree as to the nature of false comedians. This suggests that all false comedians are essentially alike, and one can make firm, fairly specific generalizations about them. True comedians are likely to be as different from each other as Huck and Jim are from Quixote and Sancho, and one must proceed cautiously in making any generalizations about them. In the second half of this chapter I examine two modern American writers who are so very different that relatively few people are willing to join me in admiring both at once, yet both are true comedians, E. B. White and Henry Miller.

In 1614 one who signed himself Alonso Fernandez de Avellaneda took his place among the great damned fools of all time by publishing a book that claimed to be a sequel to part 1 of *Don Quixote*. Nobody but a fool would be fat-headed enough to think that he could match the lovely subtleties of Cervantes' book, and only a genuine damned fool would then go out of his way to mock Cervantes for his crippled left hand, the result of wounds suffered while fighting with conspicuous bravery in Spain's greatest naval triumph. Perhaps rumor or wishful thinking had persuaded Avellaneda that he was safe to carry on in such fashion, for it had been nine years since part 1 was published and Cervantes was close to fifty-eight at that time.

But in 1614 Cervantes was very much alive; in fact, he was deep into the writing of his own authentic sequel to part 1. In his prologue to part 2, which was published in 1615, he asked his reader to convey a message to Avellaneda:

> If you by chance should come to know him, tell him on my behalf that I do not hold it against him; for I know what temptations the devil has to offer, one of the greatest of which consists in putting it into a man's head that he can write a book and have it printed and thereby achieve as much fame as he does money and acquire as much money as he does fame; in confirmation of which I would have you, in your own witty and charming manner, tell him this tale.
>
> There was in Seville a certain madman whose madness assumed one of the drollest forms that ever was seen in this world. Taking a hollow reed sharpened at one end, he would catch a dog in the street or somewhere else; and, holding one of the animal's legs with his foot and raising the other with his hand, he would fix his reed as best he could in a certain part, after which he would blow the dog up, round as a ball. When he had it in this condition he would give it a couple of slaps on the belly and let it go, remarking to the bystanders, of whom there were always plenty, ''Do your Worships think, then, that it is so easy a thing to inflate a dog?'' So you might ask, ''Does your Grace think that it is so easy a thing to write a book?'' (P. 506)

Imagine the look on Avellaneda's face as he tried to sort that one out.

However, there was a lot more than that to Cervantes' response. Avellaneda, with the dazzling ineptitude of his kind, had walked right into the middle of Cervantes' most powerful concerns.

Very early in part 1 Cervantes had discovered that his mad, idealistic knight required the company of an unlettered, earthy squire—that is, he had discovered that the book required two deeply contrasting figures to do justice to the complex, paradoxical truths of his comic vision. Yet, as part 1 went on, as Quixote and Sancho had more and more adventures, and especially as they had more and more opportunity to talk about the adventures they had had, the contrasting figures moved closer and closer together. One feels that this gradual merging was as much a surprise and revelation to Cervantes as it is to the reader. Perhaps (only perhaps) that is why the last half of part 1 is clogged with long, interpolated tales having nothing to do with Quixote and Sancho though the first half had maintained a remarkably steady narrative flow: Cervantes was playing for time, so to speak, to understand what he was creating.

That is speculation. But certainly in the seven or eight years between the publication of part 1 and the writing of part 2 Cervantes came to a deeper understanding of the relationship between the pair. From the very beginning of the second book they are collaborators, partners in a single enterprise, rather than contrasting figures in a scheme of things. Each has a role to play that he plays to the hilt, but each borrows freely from the other's role, Quixote using Sanchoesque proverbs, Sancho attempting Quixotic flights of rhetoric. This becomes especially marked in the last part of the book when Quixote's energies are flagging. Sancho takes the lead in solving the "problem" of releasing Dulcinea from enchantment; he retires to the woods and lays the required 3300 lashes on some trees instead of on his own back while Quixote stays behind, cautioning him not to injure himself. In the first book Cervantes defined Quixote and Sancho by contrasting them with each other; in the second, he defines them by contrasting them, as a pair, with the rest of the world. In particular, he contrasts them with the duke and the duchess, a pair of false comedians, wealthy fools who use their money, their power, and their servants to arrange a long series of "jokes" that are intended to provoke the madness and drollery of the knight and the squire.

That is the theme that Avellaneda walked right into with his inept, mean-spirited sequel. Having decided at the beginning of his work on part 2 that Quixote and Sancho would keep meeting people who had read part 1, Cervantes had no trouble at all opening up his fiction to include the existence of the false sequel. The actual damned fool, Avellaneda, joins the fictional damned fools, the duke and the duchess, as prime examples of false comedians, while Cervantes joins the blessed fools, the true comedians Quixote and Sancho.

Of the figures used in defining the theme of the false comedians the duke and the duchess loom largest, though more accurately the actions they precipitate take the largest amount of space, for they themselves have relatively little to do and as individuals they are only sketchily characterized. Meeting with Quixote and Sancho by accident, they invite them to be their guests at their estate and decide to humor them in every way in the hope of eliciting for their own private pleasure the fantastical behavior and speeches that had delighted the readers of part I. When they are content merely to provide a setting, Quixote and Sancho respond with some of their finest humor. Thus, at dinner the first night Sancho tells, with his characteristic excess of detail and repetition, a story that neatly deflates the polite maneuvering between the duke and Quixote over who shall sit at the head of the table; Quixote unleashes his superb rhetoric to reprove a stuffy churchman who has condemned his "foolish," "addle-pated," "silly" dedication to knight-errantry. But the duke and the duchess are not content to trust in the flow of time and chance; they must arrange things. They have already encouraged their servants to play tricks on their guests, most of which are as notably unfunny as the effort to wash Sancho's hair and beard in foul dishwater, and they themselves "produce" (using the word as Hollywood does) a pageant about magicians and enchanters that culminates in a lengthy piece of poor verse declaring that Dulcinea can be released from her enchantment only by Sancho's giving himself 3300 lashes. It is as elaborate and as expensive and as vapid as any pageant in a Hollywood musical. But the ducal pair, like their Hollywood counterparts, are dazzled by their own dullness and go on to more elaborate productions, most notably a complicated charade in which Sancho is given an "island" to govern and then is besieged with trick questions and crude practical jokes that are designed to make him look foolish.

The "jokes" of the duke and the duchess and their retinue are meanly self-centered as well as trite and crude. If the affair of the governorship ends with Sancho badly bruised, that does not bother the duke and the duchess at all, and they are not greatly disturbed when another practical joke goes awry and costs Quixote five days in bed as a result of having been painfully clawed in the face by a cat.

But their wrath is aroused when they are cheated of the pleasure of watching Quixote joust to defend the honor of a duenna's daughter because a lackey decides that he would rather marry the girl than fight. As we find out later, after Quixote leaves they forbid the marriage and have the lackey given a hundred blows with a club for disobeying them.

As long as they are guests at the estate Quixote and Sancho are remarkably patient and forbearing, but as soon as they set forth on the open road again, Quixote gives eloquent statement to his own and the reader's feelings: " 'Freedom,' he said, turning to Sancho, 'is one of the most precious gifts that the heavens have bestowed on men; with it the treasures locked in the earth or hidden in the depths of the sea are not to be compared; for the sake of freedom, as for the sake of honor, one may and should risk one's life, and captivity, on the other hand, is the greatest evil that can befall a human being. . . .' " Sancho replies, in comic character as always: "For all that your Grace says, we ought to be duly grateful for the two hundred gold crowns which the duke's majordomo handed to me in a little purse and which I now carry next to my heart as a kind of soothing plaster against a time of need; for we are not always going to find castles where they will entertain us, and sometimes we are likely to come upon inns where they will give us a beating" (pp. 882–83). That is all they have to say on the subject; they just plunge right into a series of their own characteristic adventures.

But the critical implications are clear, even though Cervantes, like his characters, is too busy getting on with the next thing, as well as too considerate of his reader's right to think for himself, to underline and analyze. The highest values of the true comedian are freedom and honor, though his definition of honor is very much his own. False comedians have no concern for freedom; they are so busy arranging things to provide for their own entertainment that they have no awareness of the otherness of others. And though they may be as full of the world's honors as dukes and duchesses, they are devoid of any sense of honor. They claim to love jokes, but if they can help it the joke is never on them. The true comedian does not love a joke, he lives it; he himself is his own best joke. That explains why the humor of false comedians is so trite. They want jokes that are known, that can be controlled and arranged, that are safe to handle. The true comedian delights in the hitherto unknown, or at least unexpected, joke; for him it is an adventure.

If the duke and the duchess loom large in part 2, providing the most detailed representation of false comedians, Avellaneda looms small, occasioning brief but subtle reflections on the theme. Apart from the preface, nearly all the commentary on Avellaneda and his false sequel is contained in parts of chapters 59 and 72. In chapter 59 the chief emphasis is on the gross inadequacy of Avellaneda's portrayals of Quixote and Sancho. Clearly, he could not possibly follow Quixote into that "vague realm between sound sense and madness" in which he flourishes, and he was too coarse himself to do justice to the "drollness" of a peasant who loves to eat and drink and who takes great pride in being a squire to a mad knight-errant.

That primary criticism is clear and simple, but in this book—in the authentic *Don Quixote*—nothing stays simple very long, even though everything always looks simple. For one thing, in this chapter Cervantes gives particularly heavy stress to the "fact" that Cid Hamete Benengeli is the original author of *Don Quixote;* Cervantes claims only to have put into fluent Spanish the literal translation that he had commissioned from an anonymous translator of the Moor's manuscript. In doing this, he is mocking Avellaneda's failure to give credit where credit is due; he is also reminding us that the plagiarist was either too stupid or too egotistical to take advantage of a superbly well-chosen narrative point of view.

More important, chapter 59 benefits from the fundamental complication in part 2: Quixote and Sancho, and nearly everyone they meet, know about the books that have been written about them and are in a position to criticize the authors. This obliterates the usual boundary lines drawn between fiction and reality with fascinating results in every aspect of the book. (I do not know how others respond, but when I am reading part 2 and keep discovering fictional characters who have had the same experience I have just had, the experience of reading part 1, I begin to get the odd but bracing feeling that I, too, am a character in Cervantes' fiction. In my dreamier moments I suspect the book is reading me.) In the particular matter of the criticism of Avellaneda as a false comedian, I take this to mean that the true comedian does not hold himself superior to his characters and his material; he submits to their right to judge and even to contradict him. It is the mark of a false comedian, whether he is a writer like Avellaneda or a ''producer'' like the duke and the duchess, to insist that his audience separate him from the comedy he is making. The false comedian keeps signaling, ''This is only a joke; I am only pretending that this is about me or about you.'' The true comedian keeps insisting that his comedy is the literal truth even when it is perfectly obvious that that is a bald-faced lie. Obviously, Quixote and Sancho are fantastical characters; obviously, their adventures are purely fictional. Yet Cervantes swears to us that all of this is true history, and we believe him, if we have any sense. For, in a way, all of this is as true as any narrative statement can be; but even if it is not, we cannot learn from it until we grant the characters and their actions a reality equal to our own.

The second scene involving Avellaneda's book, chapter 72, reinforces all of the criticisms implicit in the first scene, and does so with high, Cervantean flair. Quixote and Sancho meet Don Alvaro Tarfe, a character out of Avellaneda's version. After some pleasant conversation he agrees to make out an affadavit swearing that they do not in any way resemble the Don Quixote and the Sancho Panza he had met before. He concludes, with a little help from Quixote, that he must have been enchanted when he met and accepted those other pitiful imposters.

So much for Avellaneda. Appropriately enough, that was only a pen name. We need not worry about what his ''real'' name was, for like all false comedians he was only a poor invention. False comedians may be born and die and pay taxes and so forth, but they do not touch reality.

There are three other minor characters in part 2 who affect the theme of the false comedian—Bachelor Sanson Carrasco, the man from Quixote's village who decides to cure him of his madness by defeating him in battle; Don Diego de Miranda, the prudent gentleman of La Mancha whom Quixote dubs ''the Knight of the Green-colored Greatcoat''; and Don Antonio Moreno of Barcelona, ''a gentleman of wealth and discernment who was fond of amusing himself in an innocent and kindly way'' (p. 914). Don Antonio and Don Diego stand in contrast to the duke and the duchess. Like them, Don Antonio has been delighted by part 1, lavishes hospitality upon Quixote and Sancho, and even plays some tricks upon them in order to savor their behavior; but there is a crucial difference between him and those false comedians, his tricks are free of cruelty and he has a tender regard for Quixote and Sancho. He cannot make very good comedy himself, but he appreciates good comedy and respects those who can make it. Don Diego is an ideal country gentleman. He has never heard of Quixote—he is the only literate character in part 2 who has not read part 1—but even if he had, he is much too courteous and too sober to indulge in practical jokes. He is astonished, as any sensible man must be, by Quixote's extravagances, but he is also impressed, as any intelligent man should be, by the wisdom of his discourse where matters of knight-errantry are not concerned. Not a comedian himself, he pays his puzzled respect to the true comedian.

Thematically, the Bachelor is a complex figure. He responds so strongly to Quixote's ''madness'' that he imitates it. Early in part 2 he dresses up, quite elaborately, as the Knight of the Mirrors and seeks Quixote to do battle with him. He assumes that he will defeat Quixote, and he plans to exact a pledge from Quixote to return to his village for a year so that he may be cured of his madness. But when things go wrong and Quixote unseats him, it becomes clear that there is more vanity than charity in the Bachelor; he promptly declares that he will try again, this time giving Quixote a good, revengeful thrashing. His second effort, dressed as the Knight of the White Moon, is successful, mostly because his horse is so much faster and stronger than Rocinante, and he exacts Quixote's pledge to return home. To this point the Bachelor is a false comedian, a man who cannot play with mock seriousness, who converts playfulness to competitiveness and therefore cannot tolerate defeat. He is one with all those admirers of professional football whose motto is "Winning is not the main thing, it is the only thing." But Cervantes' imagination is Christian; it sees repentance and change as real possibilities. When Quixote, who has returned home exhausted and dying, throws out one last imaginative possibility for his friends, to live as shepherds practicing the virtues of the pastoral life, it is the Bachelor who throws himself most enthusiastically into projecting the scheme. Bragging of his ability to compose pastoral verses and inventing names for imaginary beloveds, he joins Sancho in urging Quixote to get up from his deathbed and go out into the fields with them. Like a true comedian, the Bachelor has learned to throw himself unreservedly into foolishness for the sake of foolishness.

Though no one else has explored the theme of the false comedian as deeply and as lucidly as Cervantes has, it does appear, as I indicated at the beginning of this chapter, throughout comic literature. When Shakespeare, Fielding, Ibsen, Joyce, and the others I cited dealt with the theme, they did so openly, apparently in full awareness of what they were doing and certainly with the expectation that their audiences or their readers would comprehend the implications of their scenes and characterizations. Yet if a theme has genuine imaginative power—that is, if it speaks to or for some deep need or conviction of the imagination—it can appear in literary works without either the writer or the reader having any conscious awareness of it. Witness all of the Victorian poems, novels, and plays that seemed so innocent then and that we now see to be saturated with sexual meaning; or witness the works of many periods in which basic myths have flourished beneath the surface of awareness. The theme of the false comedian, though it does not have the compelling power of sexual yearnings or of myths of death and rebirth, can also appear in well-disguised form. The best possible illustration of this lies in the Tom Sawyer episodes in *Huckleberry Finn*.

I argue that Tom Sawyer is an image of the false comedian, fully comparable to Cervantes' duke and duchess, or at least as fully comparable as a small town, nineteenth-century American boy who seems certain to grow up to be a pillar of his community can be to a pair of seventeenth-century Spanish aristocrats. I must promptly add that Mark Twain did not want to admit to himself—in fact, could not admit—that Tom is a false comedian. Neither do most of Mark Twain's American readers. Even critics as penetrating as Lionel Trilling and T. S. Eliot have not wanted to admit it, for there is something in most of us that does not want to admit to the bitter inadequacy of Tom Sawyer. We wish he were true, but we feel he is false, damn it. Many or most of us, I suspect, duck the whole matter by following Hemingway's advice when we reread the book and skip the Tom Sawyer episode at the end.

The surest test of the falsity of the duke and the duchess is what they try to make of Quixote and Sancho; the surest test of Tom's falsity is what he does make of Huck and Jim. In Tom's presence Huck is reduced to a countrified, boyish version of the sidekick that used to flourish in second-rate Hollywood westerns—a precursor of Fuzzy Knight, Leo Carillo, and Andy Devine. With Jim the reduction is even more painful; he becomes a "darky," a boneheaded, shiftless, shuffling black servant out of a popular melodrama—the part that Stepin Fetchit used to play with cynical skill.

These reductions are clear in the opening chapters of the book, especially chapter 2 in which Tom makes Jim think that he has been bewitched while asleep under a tree. Chapter 3 offers a special aggravation: Tom leads Huck and others in their gang of boys in an attack on what he says is a group of Spaniards and "A-rabs" and camels and elephants; when the group turns out to be nothing but a Sunday school picnic, Tom loftily cites *Don Quixote,* saying it was all a matter of enchantment. Tom, like the duke and the duchess, is only pretending to have a Quixotic belief in enchanters; he is just playing a game, a nice, safe game. Huck's summary judgment of Tom's tales of enchanters and genies is sound: "It had all the marks of a Sunday school." Given Twain's own contempt for the religion of the Sunday schools, that is a harsh judgment, but Twain does nothing either then or later in the book to show that it is a judgment of Tom as well as of romances and fairy tales.

The opening chapters are offensive enough, but since Jim is not very important in them and since they function at a level where stereotyped jokes and characters are acceptable, one can be patient with them. But once Pap enters in chapter 5, his face white, "not like another man's white, but a white to make a body sick, a white to make a body's flesh crawl—a tree-toad white, a fish-belly white," the book soars, as we all know, to the highest level of art where all stereotypes, even those of slaves, are transmuted into something vibrant with individual life. Thus, it is intolerably offensive when Tom reenters the book in chapter 33, after all of those marvelous scenes of Huck and Jim together on Jackson's Island and on the raft, and again reduces Jim to the "darky" and Huck to the ignorant sidekick. From there to the end of the book eleven chapters later, we get a practically perfect exploration of the theme of the false comedian—yet there is no evidence at all that Twain was aware of what he was doing.

Twain thought he was simply combining a burlesque of the immensely popular romances by Alexandre Dumas and others with some good-natured low comedy about life on a small southern plantation. He saw Tom as an innocent vehicle for romantic notions, a high-spirited boy who could not be held responsible for the things he would do out of pure playfulness. The response he wanted, and for the most part received, is given in a footnote in the Norton Critical Edition of the text: "In these concluding chapters, the persistent horseplay may seem a cruelty toward Jim; yet here, as before, he participates in familiar antics with boys whom he trusts, although actually he could easily have escaped. The author, in this relaxed mood, employs the extravagance of comic statement and situation traditional with the frontier tall tale, but at the highest level of human understanding" (p. 202).

But Tom *is* cruel to Jim, extending his imprisonment, forcing him to submit to a variety of indignities, and making his "escape" unnecessarily dangerous. The forty dollars he finally gives him for having been such a "patient" prisoner does not excuse his cruelty any more than the two hundred gold crowns that the duke and duchess gave Sancho excuses their cruelty. Tom's humor is cruel toward everyone, not just to ex-slaves. Huck, too, is forced to be patient with Tom's schemes, Aunt Sally must suffer a plague of snakes in her house, Uncle Silas must submit to being made to look silly, and Aunt Polly must come all the way down from Hannibal because she does not get any answer to her letters.

Tom's cruelty springs from the same source as that of the duke and the duchess, vanity. We are supposed to excuse it on the ground that it is just boyish thoughtlessness, but this boy, unlike Huck and unlike Ben Rogers and the other boys in their gang, is always anxious to demonstrate his superiority to everyone about him. He does it by acting with ''style.'' Consider his scheme for freeing Jim, beginning with his scornful rejection of Huck's straightforward plan for stealing the key to the hut some night and fleeing downriver on the raft, running at night and laying up days.

> ''Wouldn't that plan work?'' Huck asks.
> ''*Work?* Why cert'nly, it would work, like rats a fighting. But it's too blame simple; there ain't nothing *to* it. What's the good of a plan that ain't no more trouble than that? It's as mild as goose-milk. Why, Huck, it wouldn't make no more talk than breaking into a soap factory.''
> I never said nothing, because I wasn't expecting nothing different; but I knowed mighty well that whenever he got *his* plan ready it wouldn't have none of them objections to it.
> And it didn't. He told me what it was, I see in a minute it was worth fifteen of mine, for style, and would make Jim just as free as mine would, and maybe get us all killed besides. (Chap. 34)

That's Tom. It is not enough to have a plan that will work; in fact, it is far more important to have one that will make people talk, one that has *style*. Tom's own plan has it. It is a mish-mash of devices lifted from the books he has read about escaping prisoners, Cellini, Casanova, the Count of Monte Cristo, and others. The devices—a rope ladder, tunnels through rock, forlorn messages, and so forth— have nothing to do with Jim's actual situation, but they do impress people. Jim is impressed, if only because he has no choice but to play along with Tom; Huck is impressed, because he can scarcely read himself and has always been impressed by bookishness; and the people around the Phelps farm are impressed, because the whole scheme is so far removed from anything that has ever happened in their simple, solidly dull lives.

Everybody talks about it afterward, just as everybody talked about *King Kong, Jaws,* and *The Towering Inferno* a few years ago and used to talk about the epics of Cecil B. DeMille. Practicing his style, Tom is even closer to a Hollywood producer than the duke and the duchess were. His own summary comment (in chapter 42) on the false adventure is apt in more ways than Twain could possibly have known: "Wasn't it bully, Aunty!" Shades of Teddy Roosevelt, twenty years before he came on the political scene!

There is only one apparent flaw in this exploration of the theme of the false comedian. Tom does get shot in the leg; thus, his comic production is not perfectly safe for him. But since bullets and death have no reality for him, he welcomes the wound in the same way that a producer welcomes a few modestly hazardous accidents when he is shooting on location: it puts a stamp of authenticity on the spectacle and thereby helps at the box office.

The big question, of course, is how in the world could Mark Twain do all of this without knowing that he was doing it? The answer, of course, is I do not know. But how could the editors of the Norton Critical Edition of *Huckleberry Finn,* like most of Twain's readers in the last hundred years, manage to avoid seeing savage criticism in the portrait of Tom Sawyer?

I do know, as we all do, that Tom Sawyer has been one of the most popular figures ever created by an American writer. Twain certainly knew it; he could tell from the sales figures for *The Adventures of Tom Sawyer,* from the efforts of theater people to get him to make or to permit a stage adaptation of the book, and from the response of audiences to his readings from the lecture platform of Tom Sawyer passages. We all know also that in Twain's imagination Tom was inextricably linked with Huck Finn; Huck appears in every book and story that Tom appears in. Tom remains a relatively constant figure, changing very little from *Tom Sawyer* to *Huckleberry Finn* to *Tom Sawyer, Detective* and *Tom Sawyer Abroad;* but there is a tremendous difference between the Huck of the raft passages and the Huck who appears in the company of Tom. Most of us tend to forget how very little there is of the real Huck—the Huck who is engraved as deeply on the imaginations of people everywhere as Don Quixote is—in the Huck of *Tom Sawyer.* We all know—or should know—that Twain was consistently ambivalent in his own attitude toward Tom. He is least troubled by that ambivalence in *Tom Sawyer,* probably because he wrote it relatively early in his career (1874–75), and perhaps, too, because he was able to think of it as a children's book. The ambivalence is most destructive in *Tom Sawyer Abroad* and *Tom Sawyer, Detective,* both of which were written in the 1890s, after so many of his crucial ambivalences had collapsed in the imagined horror of the last part of *A Connecticut Yankee,* which he finished in 1889.

I can offer no explanation of this, only a way of talking about it. That part of Twain which created the image of Huck and Jim on the raft and explored that image with depth of feeling and understanding recognized the necessity of opposing the images of the true comedian (Huck and Jim together) with an image of the false comedian (Tom). That is, he responded to the same necessity that Cervantes responded to. Like Cervantes' false comedian, Twain's stood for a much more respectable set of attitudes and way of life than did his true comedian: the false comedian always speaks for the ruling spirit of his time. But Twain could not possibly criticize his false comedian as openly, as consciously as Cervantes criticized his—and Cervantes kept his criticism fairly well masked. If Twain had cut himself off from the things that Tom Sawyer stood for, he would almost certainly have cut himself off from all of the things he had learned to strive for—a large, responsive audience, prosperity, worldly influence and power, and a respectable family life. He was a bourgeois man at a time when bourgeois ideals were flourishing; it is fashionable to sneer at them but the history of the last two hundred years testifies to their enormous power. Furthermore, if Mark Twain had rejected Tom

Sawyer he would have rejected the only fictional comic hero he had discovered who could flourish within society. Jim is a slave and is therefore excluded from society; Huck finishes his book by deciding to light out for the territory; and Hank Morgan, the Connecticut Yankee, first attempts to boss and then destroys his society in Arthurian England. Only Tom is in his society and one cannot imagine him ever being anything but in society. (Perhaps the connection between him and Teddy Roosevelt is not so accidental, after all.) Cervantes had no such problem. Quixote and Sancho may be ''mad'' and ''droll,'' but they are never outcasts. They are so thoroughly at home in their society that Quixote's advice on all social matters that do not touch on his madness is consistently wise and Sancho demonstrates that he could be a good, responsible governor. No American artist has ever solved the problem of forming an image of a true comedian who could flourish in his society. Henry Miller and others have given us images of true comedians in a community, but no one has given us one in a society. Small wonder that most of his readers have been as reluctant as Twain was to face up to the implications of the Tom Sawyer episode.

It might be helpful to note that when he was dealing with comic villains, the duke and the king, rather than with a false comedian, Mark Twain remained fully aware of what he was doing, and most of his readers seem glad to soak up the implications of his portraits of that precious pair. The villainy of villains is a less threatening subject than the falsity of false comedians.

To summarize, Cervantes and Twain agree on the essential nature of the false comedian. He is *self*-centered; everything he does is designed, finally, to gratify his ego. Consequently, he is at best callous and at worst cruel in his comic dealings with others. In other words, all of his comedy is manipulative; it is calculated and ''produced'' rather than spontaneous and free-flowing. He is acutely aware of style, but only in the most meretricious senses of that term. There is a secondhand quality to all of his imaginings; indeed, it would almost be fair to say that in place of an imagination he has an extensive knowledge of other people's comic devices and a first-class system of information retrieval. He has no deep disagreement with the powers-that-be of his world; consequently, his comedy is always safe, even though at first glance it may seem daring. The only slaves he will free have already been freed; the only apple carts he will upset have long since been turned over. The false comedian is a captive of a scheme of things who fears freedom.

It is not possible to make a comparable summary of what Cervantes and Twain say and show about the true comedian because their heroes are so very different from each other in so many different ways. To cite only one fundamental difference, Quixote and Sancho are fully formed, wholly mature men; Huck is a barely literate runaway boy and Jim a runaway slave who is just beginning to shed the limitations his status has placed on him. Perhaps it is only on the fundamental issue of freedom that Cervantes and Twain are in full agreement: true comedians delight in freedom and love those realities of the natural world in which they can be free. Of course, that makes them appear to be fools, and perhaps they really are. But true comedians are blessed fools while false comedians are damned fools. Cervantes being Christian, Quixote and Sancho are, as W. H. Auden suggested, Christian saints. Twain being pagan, the Mississippi River in *Huckleberry Finn* is a god, as Lionel Trilling suggests, and Huck and Jim live in perfect harmony with it.

Though my emphasis in the first half of this chapter was on elucidating the theme of the false comedian as it appears in *Don Quixote* and *Huckleberry Finn,* I was also demonstrating the critical usefulness of William Lynch's distinction between true and false comedians. Lynch's idea gave me a clear way of dealing with two of the major texts in comic literature. In the case of *Don Quixote* it gave me a way of understanding and explaining the structure and significance of part 2; in the case of *Huckleberry Finn* it gave me a way of accounting for the presence of the Tom Sawyer episode at the end, a presence that has been a nagging problem for critics of American literature. In the second half of this chapter I will reverse my emphasis. That is, I will argue that the concept of the true comedian has critical usefulness for dealing with bodies of work by apparently dissimilar comic artists, but I hope that the discussion will further clarify the concept.

Henry Miller and E. B. White are the two artists I will discuss. I realize that relatively few people are inclined to join me in admiring the works of both writers. Most people who admire White's essays and fiction find Miller's work sloppy, fatuous, offensive, and boring; most people who delight in Miller's essays and fiction find White's work small, safe, middle-class, and boring. And some good readers, accepting both negative judgments, would bridle at describing either writer as an artist. There is no arguing with likes and dislikes. I only argue that there is a quality one must respect in the collected works of each man and that quality is most apparent when one looks at them from a Lynchian point of view.

Although they differ about as widely as two writers can in tone and technique, White and Miller are not so totally different from each other as to render comparison preposterous. Both are comic, even funny writers. All of Miller's books reach, or at least strive to reach, a serene, comic acceptance of whatever matters they deal with, and most of them are shot through with raucous, often obscene humor. *Tropic of Cancer,* with its cheerful accounts of bars and whorehouses and its celebration of life at the very bottom of the social heap, is perfectly representative. White's work, from his single paragraph "Comments" in the "Talk of the Town" section of the *New Yorker* through his essays in *One Man's Meat* and other collections and including *Charlotte's Web* and his other children's fiction, is even more obviously comic and humorous. White is even a jokesmith of considerable skill; for years he wrote the headings and responses for the news clippings sent in by *New Yorker* readers that provide the magazine with one of its funniest and most popular features. Both take their own lives as the subject matter of their best known works. White's essays are mostly polished, reticent reflections on his past or present experience; Miller's "novels" are apparently unpolished, certainly unreticent celebrations of his own life. Yet both go well beyond the conventional boundaries of autobiography, White to create realistic fantasies for children and Miller to write pungent literary and social criticism. Both are Americans of roughly the same age; Miller was born in 1890 and White in 1899. But since Miller's Brooklyn was a world apart from White's Mount Vernon, New York, I do not attach much significance to that similarity. However, I would give considerable weight to the fact that they both belong squarely in the tradition of American transcendentalism—that is, they have worked out their own versions of the set of beliefs and attitudes that were first and best expressed by Emerson, Thoreau, and Whitman.

White is especially responsive to Thoreau, and that response is implicit in nearly everything he has ever written. The clearest and most comically loving statements of it are in his two essays on *Walden,* the first in *One Man's Meat* (1942) in the form of a letter to Thoreau, and the second, more elaborate one in *The Points of My Compass* (1962) under the title "A Slight Sound at Evening." But I doubt that anyone who was not soaked in Thoreau's work could have written *Charlotte's Web* (1952), for it derives its power and charm as much from White's close, patient, accurate observation of the behavior of the animals in his barn in Maine as it does from the fantasy he created about a spider saving a pig from slaughter by spinning words into her web above his pen. It would be too much to claim that White could have been comfortable in the actual presence of Thoreau—few people ever could relax in the presence of that "regular hair-shirt of a man," to use White's phrase—but he has certainly taken steady delight in the companionship of his works. He may lack Thoreau's intellectual brilliance, but he shares his delight in the microcosmic and in sentences that combine low facts with high feelings while remaining wholly speakable. Though his reticence does not seem to be as deeply grounded in sensuality as Thoreau's asceticism was, it does seem natural, not the least bit prissy.

Miller's transcendentalism is as evident as White's, though a surprising number of readers have managed not to notice it, perhaps because they do not expect to find a transcendentalist with his fly unzipped. The quotation from Emerson that serves as the epigraph for *Tropic of Cancer* (1934) ought in itself to be sufficient evidence:

"These novels will give way, by and by, to diaries or autobiographies—captivating books, if only a man knew how to choose among what he calls his experiences that which is truly his experience, and how to record truth truly." One could argue that *Tropic of Cancer* and all of Miller's other "quaint autobiographical romances" (his term for them) grow out of that passage. There is plenty of Thoreau in Miller, too; one can see that plainly in *Big Sur and the Oranges of Hieronymous Bosch* (1957), for his whole stay at Big Sur was something like an experiment in Thoreauvian living, albeit an experiment forced on him by dire economic necessity. Yet it is Whitman he is closest to, not only in his celebration of sexuality, but in his cheerful, easy relation with the vulgar and in his willingness to sound a barbaric yawp. Miller, who was fond of describing himself as "only a Brooklyn boy," could, I think, have been comfortable in the actual presence of the "garrulous," "loafing," "rough" Whitman.

To state the similarity in Lynch's terms, both White and Miller are true comedians. That is, both are flooded by a comic remembrance of life, and their very different remembrances are "somehow one in some kind of love of the human and some kind of refusal to be ashamed of human parentage." Both trust in the finite and delight in the concrete; neither has much regard for categories or for any of the other works of univocal minds and imaginations. Both have the courage and the gaiety to be hopeful. Having asked a lot of themselves, they do not strike cozy little bargains with their readers. Of course, White is a polite, deeply courteous man and Miller a natural-born outcast; so the language and works of the one are always controlled and unshocking, while the language and works of the other always tend toward the outrageous. No book of White's has ever been banned in Boston or anywhere else, and some of Miller's—*Sexus,* especially—were banned in places where they had never banned books before. Also, of course, each flirted with his appropriate form of disaster: White nearly became mired in the swamp of middle-class attitudes and egotism in the same way that his friend and one-time collaborator Thurber did, and Miller was perpetually in danger of being trapped, as so many of his admirers have been, in some attractively disreputable way of asserting his independence. Yet both managed through long, productive careers to remain faithful to themselves and to their own versions of the basic Emersonian faith in the holiness of the individual and of the natural world.

For a tag to put on White's version I go to the first essay in *One Man's Meat,* "Removal," in which he expressed his fear of television: "Together with the tabs, the mags, and the movies, it will insist that we forget the primary and the near in favor of the secondary and the remote." As his letters and a few excerpts from his youthful journals show, White's impulse has always been to favor the primary and the near; and relatively early in his career he realized that the small event, the ordinary person, and the commonplace thing are superior in interest, wisdom, and value to the abstract idea, the important person, and the rare thing. That theme is implicit in his first books, *The Lady Is Cold* (1929), a collection of verse, and *Is Sex Necessary?* (1929), a spoof of heavy sex books that he wrote with James Thurber. It runs with increasing explicitness and increasing complexity through his writing in the thirties and forties and finds fullest expression in *Charlotte's Web* and in the essays gathered in *The Points of My Compass.* The theme explains why he was attracted to children's books and why he put so much of himself and of his ideas about writing in revising for publication in 1959 *The Elements of Style,* the "little" book on composition that White's instructor at Cornell, Professor William Strunk, had originally published in 1918. It even explains that apparent anomaly in White's works, *The Wild Flag* (1946), a collection of pieces that he had written during the war for "The Talk of the Town" section of the *New Yorker* advocating a form of supranational government. Seeing the war as a terrible eruption of the secondary and the remote in the lives of people everywhere, White tried to imagine a form of government that would encourage people to identify with both their own localities and the entire world rather than with a nation state. For once, his theme called for him to do some disciplined abstract thinking; naturally, he was not very good at it.

Miller's theme is harder to state neatly, perhaps because it turned out to be a bigger and much more demanding one, yet it is similar to White's. Two quotes from *Tropic of Cancer* will serve to bracket it: "I have no money, no resources, no hopes. I am the happiest man alive" (p. 1). "I love everything that flows" (p. 232). The theme seems to have come to him some time during the early twenties while he was working as the New York employment manager of Western Union. His life was in chaos: the work made no sense at all, his marriage was breaking up, night after night he was making wild sexual forays, and though he desperately wanted to become a writer, he either did not know how to try or did not dare to. Finally, he realized that everything that happened in the world of the telegraph company (the province of the secondary and the remote) truly was insane, utterly senseless and never more so than when it was claiming to be reasonable, and that everything that happened in his personal world made some kind of sense, because it was the province of the primary and the near, the organic and the fluid. "Sink or swim!" was the cry of the telegraph company, and Miller saw that *everybody* sank, no matter how hard they swam. "Float!" is the imperative of the personal world, and Miller saw that everybody could float, if only they stopped worrying about things like money, resources, and hopes.

Miller floated out of the telegraph company readily enough, but it took him the better part of ten years to find the way of writing that his theme and his experience demanded. It is no wonder, for the demands are fiercely difficult. For one thing, he had to open up his writing to the "obscene," using that poor, bedeviled term as Miller uses it in "Obscenity and the Law of Reflection" (*Remember to Remember*, 1947), not as the courts do. That is much, much harder to do than the censorious would have us believe. Even a writer as great as D. H. Lawrence failed at it in *Lady Chatterley's Lover*, and James Joyce's attempts in *Ulysses* were only tentative and inconclusive. Sheer pornography is simple enough, but the trick is to manage the obscene without destroying all of the other qualities of a work of art. Miller was the first writer to do it in any sustained way in modern English prose; and even with his work as model, relatively few have managed the trick in the last twenty years, though many have certainly tried. His feat is all the more impressive when you realize that he had to write *Tropic of Cancer* and the other obscene books which followed it in the thirties and forties in the certain knowledge that they could not be published in any English-speaking country. All of the sanctimonious people who have accused Miller of pandering to the prurient interests of the public in order to make money should realize that he had to pay the price of twenty-five years of poverty for the privilege of freeing his work from sexual taboos. The pandering and the money-making have been done by those popular novelists (Kathleen Winsor, Harold Robbins, and their clones) who have drawn with exquisite accuracy the line between titillating the middle classes and arousing their censorious ire.

But Miller's theme made other severe demands upon him, too. It required him to give his intellect and his imagination the same kind of floating freedom he gave his appetites—that is, he also had to open up his writing to surrealistic flights of images and to associational (or alogical) kinds of arguing. And finally, he had to get his books to hold together without imposing a purposeful structure on them; it had to happen by apparent accident.

Through bad times and good, war and peace, famine and feast, Miller was as faithful to his theme as White has been to his. It is as solidly there in his *Book of Friends* (1976) as it is in *Tropic of Cancer* (1934); and it is as solidly there in books that are totally free of the obscene, such as *The Colossus of Maroussi* (1941), as it is in books that are full of the most pungent obscenity, such as *Sexus* (1949). His readers, as he observes in the opening paragraph of *The World of Sex* (1940, 1957), split into factions over the results: some love the early and/or the obscene works; some the later and/or the speculative works. Miller, who was sometimes known as The Happy Rock, was unconcerned. He lived by the light of his beliefs and he withheld no part of himself in his written work.

White, too, has put his ideas to the test of living by them. An account of his life would scarcely serve as a script for a movie about a writer who has suffered for his art, but in order to get his work done he has more than once had to cut loose from some nicely sheltered mooring. The crucial cut was the one he made in 1938, when he quit his full-time job with the *New Yorker,* persuaded his wife, Katharine, to give up her editorship there, and moved his family to a saltwater farm in Brooklin, Maine. He quit because he knew his writing required him to—the shortness of the ''Comment'' form was becoming stifling, the magazine's requirement that he write them in the first person plural was frustrating, and the weekly deadlines were turning him into a kind of mechanic. Plainly, he did not know what he was getting into by going to Maine; he just knew that he should get away from the city and its excessively familiar demands on him and submit to something like a Thoreauvian test of his beliefs, a saltwater farm in Maine being a married man's equivalent of a shanty on Walden Pond. He could not have known, though he may have suspected, that he would find huge chunks of his best material there. Certainly it was not until after he had committed himself to the venture—which he first thought of as a sabbatical year—that he reached an agreement with *Harper's* to write a monthly column under the title ''One Man's Meat.'' He was attracted to it because it gave him more room to work in (four typewritten pages) and the chance to write in the first person singular. In the four and a half years that he wrote the column he resuscitated the supposedly dead form of the personal essay and mastered it as few people ever have.

Good as White's essays are, *Charlotte's Web* is his best work—his most concrete, most comprehensive, most subtle, most fully imagined embodiment of his fundamental theme. It is also a deep, sustained exploration of some of the chief recurrent images of comic literature. It is especially concerned with the comic image of time and change, but it also encompasses a gentle mockery of logic and of willful, purposeful people, an implicit rejection of wishful thinking, and a celebration of playfulness. Of course, it is a book written first for children, and as anybody this side of Lewis Carroll could have told him, White was crazy to mold an ambitious work of art in that form. I imagine that White, like Miller, would save himself considerable trouble and just plead guilty to the charge. But in his defense I observe that in a world that at one time or another has treated *Gulliver's Travels, Moby-Dick,* and *Huckleberry Finn* as children's books, there is something satisfying about writing a book explicitly for children and letting critics catch up when they can with its artistry. More important, artists cannot be choosers; they have to do the work that wants to be done by them, not the work that sensible people think they ought to do. American writers have more trouble than most in this respect; our literature is full of books that are formally very odd indeed. Even Henry James with his exquisite sense of form was driven to make such odd-seeming experiments as *The Awkward Age* and Ernest Hemingway to see, in *Green Hills of Africa,* "whether the shape of a country and the pattern of a month's action can, if truly presented, compete with a work of the imagination."

Charlotte's Web is about life in the great good place, the cellar of Zuckerman's barn. The chief personages in the microcosmic society of that place are Wilbur, a pig who had been the runt of his litter; Charlotte A. Cavatica, a grey spider about the size of a gumdrop; Templeton, a rat; a goose, a gander, and seven goslings; an old sheep and an assortment of other sheep and lambs; and Fern Arable, an eight-year-old girl who sits very quietly on a stool outside Wilbur's pen, watching and listening to the talk of the others. Fern had raised Wilbur through the first five weeks of his life in order to save him from the terrible "injustice" of immediate slaughter, which is the common fate of runtlings. The central problem of the small society is to save Wilbur from slaughter, which is the common fate of pigs that have been reared to full growth. That difficult problem is solved by Charlotte, with some unenthusiastic help from Templeton. She does it by writing—that is, by weaving words into her web above Wilbur's stall by the manure pile. First, she writes, "SOME PIG"; then, "TERRIFIC" and "RADIANT"; and finally, "HUMBLE." The first message is entirely Charlotte's; the last three she takes from words on scraps of paper brought to her by Templeton in return for a guarantee of free food from Wilbur's trough. Her writing works exactly as she intends it to; it persuades the adults in the larger, more powerful society surrounding the barn that Wilbur is much too special a pig to slaughter.

The chief personages in the larger society are Fern's parents, her older brother Avery, her aunt and uncle, the Zuckermans (who bought Wilbur when he was five weeks old), Zuckerman's hired hand, Lurvy, and a neighborhood boy named Henry Fussy, who will eventually serve to draw Fern out of the society of the barn and into the larger society. The chief characteristic of these personages is their gullibility. "If I can fool a bug," thinks Charlotte, "I can surely fool a man. People are not as smart as bugs" (p. 67). Her judgment is confirmed with charming completeness when Zuckerman tells his wife of the first message:

> "It says, 'Some Pig,' just as clear as clear can be. There can be no mistake about it. A miracle has happened and a sign has occurred here on earth, right on our farm, and we have no ordinary pig."
>
> "Well," said Mrs. Zuckerman, "it seems to me you're a little off. It seems to me we have no ordinary *spider*."
>
> "Oh, no," said Zuckerman. "It's the pig that's unusual. It says so, right there in the middle of the web."
>
> "Maybe so," said Mrs. Zuckerman. "Just the same, I intend to have a look at that spider."
>
> "It's just a common grey spider," said Zuckerman.
>
> They got up, and together they walked down to Wilbur's yard. "You see, Edith? It's just a common grey spider."
>
> Wilbur was pleased to receive so much attention. Lurvy was still standing there, and Mr. and Mrs. Zuckerman, all three, stood for about an hour, reading the words on the web over and over, and watching Wilbur. (Pp. 80–81)

The only adult who realizes that any spider's web is a miracle, even without words woven in it, is Dr. Dorian. He does not know how a young spider can spin a web without instructions from anyone, and he certainly does not understand how there could be any writing in a spider's web. "Doctors are supposed to understand everything," he says. "But I don't understand everything, and I don't intend to let it worry me" (p. 110).

The chief characteristic of the personages of the society in the barn cellar is an unanalytical delight in the progression of their days. They are totally immersed in the primary and the near, wholly free from concern about the secondary and the remote. Consequently, they are wiser than even Dr. Dorian; they do not need to *understand* anything, and so do not have to resolve not to worry about not understanding. Further, they are naturally gifted at doing the things they have to do, Charlotte at making webs and trapping flies, Wilbur at slurping down food and at sleeping on the warmth of the manure pile, Templeton at constructing runs so that he can move about without being seen, and the goose at sitting on a clutch of eggs until they hatch. Fern qualifies for membership in this society because she is a child and exercises a child's gift for wonder. The only thing they do not accept about their lives in the barn is the slaughter, ordained by economic considerations, of Wilbur. More accurately, Wilbur rebels against it because he wants to stay alive in his comfortable manure pile with all his friends around him, and Charlotte determines to save him, as Fern had done earlier, because she likes Wilbur; the others go along with them.

If the bulk of the action occurs in the great, good place, the barn cellar, the climactic scene occurs in the next best place, the county fair. There, in the spirit of festivity, the two societies can come together, almost as one. Charlotte writes her last word, HUMBLE. She explains that " 'humble' has two meanings. It means 'not proud' and it means 'near the ground.' That's Wilbur all over. He's not proud and he's near the ground" (p. 140). Wilbur is saved because he is awarded a special prize of twenty-five dollars and a bronze medal, suitably engraved, for attracting so many people to the fair. No one could ever convert such a pig into ham and bacon.

Also, Charlotte completes her "*magnum opus,*" an egg sac containing 514 eggs. That brings her, of course, to the verge of death, a fact that she accepts with equanimity. However, it drives Wilbur into panic, until he gets the idea of carrying the egg sac back to the barn with him, so he can at least have the company of Charlotte's children. The book does not so much end as fade out in a chapter suggesting the years that follow with their repeating cycles of the birth and death of Charlotte's descendants. "Wilbur never forgot

Charlotte. Although he loved her children and grandchildren dearly, none of the new spiders ever quite took her place in his heart. She was in a class by herself. It is not often that someone comes along who is a true friend and a good writer. Charlotte was both'' (p. 184).

A number of alleged adults, such as White's publishers and Anne Carroll Moore, the head of the children's section of the New York Public Library and an influential critic, objected to bringing death so powerfully into a book written for children, but to the best of my knowledge, no children have objected. They might get a bit teary-eyed, but they do not object. They know as well as White does that spiders die at the end of the summer. And Charlotte is indeed a spider, a little more gifted and a great deal more articulate than most spiders, but nonetheless, a spider.

That is White's remarkable achievement in the book; through all the fantasy his spider remains a spider, his pig a pig, his rat a rat, and his goose a goose. White rightly, and proudly, insisted on that in his various negotiations, or battles, with people wanting to make a movie of *Charlotte's Web*. He would not even consider an offer from Walt Disney, because Disney always made animals dance to *his* tune and White preferred them to dance to *their* tune. As he told the Czech moviemaker Gene Deitch (who apparently did not listen), *Charlotte's Web* is an appreciative story, not a moral tale.

> It celebrates life, the seasons, the goodness of the barn, the beauty of the world, the glory of everything. But it is essentially amoral, because animals are essentially amoral, and I respect them, and I think this respect is implicit in the tale. I discovered, quite by accident, that reality and fantasy make good bedfellows. I discovered that there was no need to tamper in any way with the habits and characteristics of spiders, pigs, geese, and rats. No ''motivation'' is needed if you remain true to life and true to the spirit of fantasy. (*Letters*, p. 613)

Before White started to write the book he spent a year carefully studying spiders, both in books and in his own barn. And he learned from them. Or, if you would prefer to put it more reasonably, he learned how to perceive and to portray animals in such a way as to make them reflect qualities and concerns that are humanly important without doing violence to their own qualities. This permitted him to write of sentiment without sentimentalizing his characters. More important, it allowed him to "hear" the finest short statement he ever made of his central theme, Charlotte's lullaby for Wilbur:

> Sleep, sleep, my love, my only,
> Deep, deep, in the dung and the dark;
> Be not afraid and be not lonely!
> This is the hour when frogs and thrushes
> Praise the world from the woods and the rushes.
> Rest from care, my one and only,
> Deep in the dung and the dark! (P. 104)

As a true comedian, White followed his theme out to the barn and down to the level of childhood; as an artist, he made a work of art in that place and on that level.

Miller, too, was a true comedian. His autobiographical romances are forceful explorations of the dimensions and images that Lynch identifies in that key passage at the head of his chapter on comedy:

> The difference between the dimensions at which tragedy and comedy operate are not easy to locate or describe. But one thing is certain. They both live and imagine at a level far below the first and superficial surfaces of man.
>
> The greatest tribute that can be paid to comedy is that its images are as deep but not as painful as those of tragedy (and altogether different from what we today call entertainment). It gets below all the categories within which the most of life is spent and destroys the most of these categories (the rich, the proud, the mighty, the beautiful, the style, the Joneses) in its descent. In this descent it discovers a kind of rock-bottom reality in man, the terrain of Falstaff and Sancho Panza, which is profoundly and funnily unbreakable, which has no needs above itself. It seems to be the most inherently confident rung of the finite. It is ugly *and* strong. (P. 91)

That descent to rock bottom and the subsequent ascent to the empyrean that is powered by the discoveries at rock bottom is the central subject of Miller's work. My own choice for the best single work on this recurring, repeating process of descent and ascent is *Tropic of*

Capricorn (1939); others—most notably, Norman Mailer (*Genius and Lust,* 1976) and Ihab Hassan (*The Literature of Silence,* 1967)— would choose *Tropic of Cancer,* and Miller himself frequently cited *The Colossus of Maroussi* as his best book. The two *Tropic*s and *Colossus* are inconveniently long and complex for my purposes here; the section of *Big Sur and the Oranges of Hieronymous Bosch* (pp. 275–385) entitled "Paradise Lost" provides a more manageable, clear example of the true comedian at work on his basic theme. (It was first published in 1956 as a separate book under the title *A Devil in Paradise.*)

In "Paradise Lost" Miller shows himself trapped by his own foolish optimism. He decides in 1947 to rescue Conrad Moricand, an acquaintance from the late thirties in Paris, from desperate poverty in Switzerland by bringing him to California to live with him and his family in their cramped, rickety cabin in Big Sur. Miller thinks it is a brilliant idea; his wife is skeptical because Moricand had never been a close friend, not even a kindred spirit. But it is enough for Miller that Moricand had given him a book he came to treasure, Balzac's *Seraphita.* Anyway, Miller still believes that "there are no limits to what one person can do for another" (p. 287). Moricand soon teaches him better.

Two men could scarcely be more opposite. Miller is impulsive, gregarious, disorderly, earthy, passionate, and deeply involved in writing *The Rosy Crucifixion.* Moricand is cold, fastidious, proud, demanding, addicted to codeine, and deeply involved in occult learning, especially astrology. Moricand is the meticulous man carried to the nth degree: his writing table has everything laid out just so, with his block of specially cut writing paper always resting slantwise on a triangular ruler with pen, ink, and freshly sharpened pencils alongside. He cannot use anything but Yardley's talcum powder and hates to smoke anything but French cigarettes. Even fresh air is too unruly for him; he has his bedroom so tightly sealed that the oil lamp cannot burn properly. While Miller is upstairs during the day writing *Plexus* in long, furious bursts of typing, Moricand is in his room fussing over astrological calculations. After dinner, Moricand holds forth, in

French because he refuses to learn English, on the subjects which interest him—his past, the wisdom of astrology, and the superiority of European civilization to American barbarism.

The differences that first seem to be merely temperamental quickly become philosophical. Miller is curious about astrology, as he is about nearly everything, because he sees it as a source of new metaphors; Moricand, who has no need for curiosity, sees it as a means of knowing certain, determined truth. Determinism is comforting to Moricand, as it is to many other intellectuals; it both relieves him of any responsibility for his own life and renders him superior to all of the ignorant clods who do not know that they are prisoners of fate. Miller loves freedom and gladly pays the price of the foolishness which it requires. Goaded by Moricand's determinism and its concomitant contempt for democracy, Miller proclaims that he is an American and glad of it; the man who had just a few years before written a book describing America as an "air-conditioned nightmare" teaches his two-year-old daughter to sing "Yankee Doodle." He is also goaded into one of the tightest, clearest statements he has made of his transcendentalism (pp. 314–26), which rests on the conviction that "what we need to discover is what *it* wishes, call *it* life, mind, God, whatever you please" (p. 324). The intellect, Miller believes, is of very little use in that effort to discover because "the intellect is the product of the ego" (p. 322) and because it deals in knowledge and wisdom. "The love of truth has nothing to do with knowledge or wisdom; it's beyond their domains" (p. 322).

Miller and his way of taking life goad Moricand; so does the wild beauty of Big Sur. His psychic disturbance becomes manifest in a fearful itch that transforms his legs into a mass of running sores. His Satanism becomes more open. He begins to display his pornographic drawings. "They were perverse, sadistic, sacrilegious . . ." and they were "all done with a delicate, sensitive hand, which only magnified the disgusting element of the subject matter" (p. 327). His accounts of his past become more revealing, especially his account of his nightmarish effort to make his way across the battlefields of France in the winter of 1944–1945 while carrying two valises

crammed full of his books, his writings, his diaries, and his horo-
scopes.

> "You lugged all that crap around like an elephant," I exclaimed,
> "at the risk of losing your own hide?"
> "A man doesn't throw away everything that is precious to him—just
> like that!"
> "I would!" I exclaimed.
> "But my whole life was bound up in those encumbrances."
> "You should have thrown your life away too!"
> "Not Moricand!" he replied, and his eyes flashed fire.
> Suddenly I no longer felt sorry for him, not for anything that had
> ever happened to him. (P. 341)

But the final break does not come until an evening when Moricand
has become infuriated at the playfulness of Miller's daughter at the
dinner table. Later, after the child has been put to bed, Moricand
launches into a lengthy, precisely observant tale about the time in
Paris when he followed a woman and her nine-year-old daughter
through a window-shopping tour of the Passage Jouffroy in Paris and
without a word being spoken struck a bargain to rape the child. The
rape and Moricand's glee in recalling it horrify Miller. "It was no
longer Moricand I was facing but Satan himself" (p. 363).

A few days later Moricand was out of Big Sur, and a few months
later he was out of the country. He died in Paris in August 1954 (in a
home for aged Swiss that had been founded by his own family in its
time of wealth) without a penny or a friend to his name.

American writers, especially those of transcendental persuasions,
are supposed to be lacking in any vision of evil, but Miller's
Moricand *is* evil and his portrait of him is vivid, meaningful, and
convincing. It is also appropriately free of the least touch of glam-
our. It stands with Hannah Arendt's portrait of Eichmann as a notice
of the banality, the fifth-ratedness of evil as men live it. Together,
they ought to be a sufficient warning to all the empty-headed, clever
people in our culture who are dabbling in violence, witchcraft, and
perversion. But such people are much too clever to read Hannah

Arendt, who is dead and therefore passé, or Henry Miller, who is also dead now, and who was always a fool.

Miller *was* a fool, a chump, a clown, even a horse's ass. Moricand could brag before he left the country that he had had Miller just as he could brag that he had had, in only a slightly different sense of the term, that child. It is easy to exploit a fool or to rape a child. Furthermore, Miller also suffered at Big Sur, not from an itch that finally caused his testicles to swell to the size of cantaloupes, but from a marriage that was falling apart in a series of senseless, bitter quarrels. But though Moricand could say of Big Sur when he first saw it, *"C'est un vrai paradis,"* he could not stand to live in it because it was not right for him; he would have had to change some part of his precious self. Miller was certain that Big Sur was paradise and knew that if he was not happy there it was somehow his own foolish fault. Neither valises full of papers nor the absence of Yardley's talcum powder, neither the opinions of clever people nor the bitterness of a wife (who had, Miller admits, a great deal to be bitter about) would stop him from trying to "discover what *it* wishes" so that he could live in full enjoyment of paradise.

Norman Mailer's comment in his preface to the excerpt from "Paradise Lost" that he includes in *Genius and Lust* is wholly appropriate:

> Miller held on through continuing poverty, and the scalding attrition of mutual marital dislike, held on for all those lonely years in Big Sur, and continued to forge his values, elaborating his sense of measure for life, and ended a long way from where he had begun, for we sense in all the quiet work of . . . this period, that we are hearing the tone of that rare writer who ends as a skilled moral craftsman. Hemingway, with his clear sense of masculine growth and deterioration, spoke more than once of how it might be necessary to sacrifice a piece of one's talent in the act of becoming a man, but it may have been Henry Miller, of all people, who took the advice. (P. 504)

Miller is, very fully, the true comedian that William Lynch describes. And Conrad Moricand is, with startling exactness, the embodiment of the qualities of mind and character that Lynch sees as hostile to true comedy in modern culture. Most especially, he represents that quality of the imagination which is so offended by the crudity and limitations of finite, time-bound life that it leaps for "magical" or "angelic" power.

A moral seems to emerge from this comparison of White and Miller: To get to paradise you should either make a horse's ass of yourself in California or listen to the conversation of spiders in Maine. To one who knows comedy that is not a particularly surprising moral, for the heroes of comedy are a notoriously foolish lot, much given to time wasting in California, in Maine, or any place else they find themselves and not the least bit inclined to take the short, purposeful way toward any goal. They believe, as Thoreau does, in being *extra*-vagant; for them, the roundabout way is the only way home.

4.
COMIC
HEROES
AND
HEROINES

The simplest and deepest, the most fundamental image of comedy, the image that is so simple that it is discovered by all comic works, so complex that no two renditions of it are identical, and so fundamental that its significance cannot be stated with any accuracy at all in direct expository prose is what I have called comedy's image of play. It would be best if we could take the term *play* as a metaphor rather than a label, a means of suggesting that what comedy celebrates, both immediately and finally, is a way of taking all of life that is like—only *like*—the way that the best of us take the best of our games at the best of our times, with a pure, empty-headed joy in doing something pointless and difficult in something like the way it really ought to be done. It is the doing that matters, not the thing done, and not the doer. To offer a metaphor for my metaphor, what comedy celebrates is very much like the lovely set of curves that Winslow Homer scratched into one of his watercolors to show a fly line in the middle of a perfect cast.

Intricately related to comedy's imperative image of play is its image of that portion of the self that deals with controlling and organizing behavior. Though this is not quite so fundamental an image, I am still struggling to find an adequate term for it. *Will* is a conventional term that we can be comfortable with, but it gives only a rough indication of the subject of the image. Moreover, since comedy deeply distrusts willful, purposeful behavior, largely, I think, because it is fueled by aggressive emotions and tends to produce destructive results, "image of will" would be an essentially negative label, pointing at what is denied or mocked rather than at what is affirmed. What comedy affirms, at least in its heroes, is an odd sort of passivity that combines a flexible yet stubborn resistance to being pushed with a general reluctance to pull. What it affirms in many of its heroines appears to be something quite different, a witty, mercurial quickness, yet the social status and the biological needs of women are so different from those of men that the difference in what is affirmed may be more apparent than real. Certainly, the qualities comedy derides are essentially the same whether the butts are men or women—arrogance, vanity, stupidity, inflexibility, and all the other faults associated with willfulness. And just as certainly, both its heroes and its heroines treat their selves, finally, with a kind of negligence—as tools to be used rather than as jewels to be treasured. In the context of their societies, comedy's heroes and heroines may appear to be self-centered, for they can be remarkably stubborn in refusing to go along with the crowd; but in the context of the actions they are intent on, they are remarkably self-negligent. It is, indeed, the doing that matters to them, not the doer.

"Passivity" is a troublesome word to have to use, especially with reference to the heroes of satiric comedies, which are more concerned with mocking than with affirming. Satiric heroes are frequently variations on the trickster figure, and they seem anything but passive as they dart here and there on the stage or in their fictional worlds. Yet a trickster hero, whether in a play by Aristophanes or a novel by Thomas Berger, rarely acts deliberately and consistently; he is a creature of impulse rather than purpose, deriding and destroying the plans of his respectably well-organized antagonists, defending himself against the will of the world instead of imposing his will on reality. For all his energy, he is finally as unconcerned with controlling his future, as passive, as any other comic hero.

The comic image of the self is so full of paradox and contradiction that direct definition of it is impossible; one must turn to examples, using at least three different comic heroes to get a fix on the image in the way that coastal pilots use at least three widely spaced landmarks to get a fix on their position. Melville's Ishmael, Fielding's Parson Adams, and Böll's Hans Schnier will serve admirably for this purpose.

It is best to begin with Ishmael, for he gives us the clearest, least ambiguous version of the image, even though he is in a novel admired for its subtle ambiguities. The clarity comes from the boldness of Melville's scheme of combining a comedy and a tragedy in a single novel; certainly it helps enormously that on every crucial point Ishmael can be contrasted with Ahab.

The tragedy, the terror of Ahab's drive toward destruction, dominates every common reader's memory of *Moby-Dick;* nonetheless, insofar as it deals with Ishmael the book is indeed a comedy. For a careful arguing of this point one can go to E. H. Rosenberry's *Melville and the Comic Spirit* (1955), but one can see it simply by separating those parts of the story that deal with Ishmael from those that focus on Ahab and by making a brief summary. Depressed, suffering from ''a damp, drizzly November'' in his soul, Ishmael decides to ship out on a whaling voyage as a common seaman. On his way to Nantucket he meets up with Queequeg, a frightfully tattooed prince of a cannibal tribe who has become an expert harpooner, and the two quickly become ''bosom friends.'' At Queequeg's insistence, Ishmael, who knows nothing about whaling, chooses the ship they will go on, the *Pequod*. Though he has been restored to good spirits by his friendship with Queequeg, Ishmael, like everyone else in the ship's company, succumbs to Ahab's furious eloquence and swears to hunt Moby Dick to his death. But unlike the others, Ishmael does not remain submissive to Ahab's purpose; calmed by such experiences as floating at the center of a school of whales and mat-making with Queequeg, Ishmael washes ''his hands and heart'' of that ''horrible oath'' while squeezing the lumps out of a tubful of sperm oil. When the final hunt begins, Ishmael goes along, as he must because he is only a common seaman and common seamen have no choice in such matters. But he alone survives the catastrophe. Having been knocked out of Ahab's boat just before the last harpoon is thrown, Ishmael clings to the life buoy from the *Pequod*, Queequeg's former coffin, until he is picked up a full twenty-four hours later by the whaler *Rachel*.

That is comedy. The protagonist passes from self-destructive despair to the self-nourishing joy of a loving relationship, loses his self-possession for a while when he gets swept up in a quest for revenge, regains his balance by renewing and enlarging his awareness of love, passes through a series of extraordinarily hazardous events over which he has no control, and finally emerges greatly chastened but unbroken. Ishmael survives.

Ishmael's story even satisfies the demand that comedy be funny, though that is an essentially irrelevant demand. Ishmael savors jokes and as narrator he supplies a great many of them. They can be as overt as his image of his own story as a brief interlude sandwiched by "those stage managers, the Fates" between the programme's spectacles:

> *Grand Contested Election for the Presidency of the United States.*
> WHALING VOYAGE BY ONE ISHMAEL.
> BLOODY BATTLE IN AFFGHANISTAN.

Or Ishmael's jokes can be as harshly sardonic as his comment at the end of an account of the dreamy pleasure of standing a watch on the masthead in fair weather: "But while this sleep, this dream is on ye, move your foot or hand an inch; slip your hold at all; and your identity comes back in horror. Over Descartian vortices you hover. And perhaps, at midday, in the fairest weather, with one half-throttled shriek, you drop through that transparent air into the summer sea, no more to rise for ever. Heed it well, ye Pantheists." His jokes can be as full of deadpan mockery as all his excursions into scholarly lore about whales, or as grinning as his account of "the strange sort of insanity" that came over him while he was squeezing the lumps out of the sperm oil. His account of his sudden friendship with Queequeg is a prolonged—and notoriously successful—put-on of delicate sensibilities toward race and sex: "Queequeg was George Washington cannibalistically developed"; and "in our heart's honeymoon, lay I and Queequeg—a cozy, loving pair." Even his account of his rescue in the closing sentences of the book is a joke, albeit of a hushed, deeply saddened sort: "On the second day, a sail drew near, nearer, and picked me up at last. It was the devious-cruising *Rachel,* that in her retracing search after her missing children, only found another orphan."

Ishmael is a hero as well as a joker. His heroism is the opposite of Ahab's. Ahab, who sees "all visible objects . . . as pasteboard

masks'' tauntingly hiding from him the nature of reality, is determined to know that reality and to demonstrate his own equality to it.
"What I've dared, I've willed; and what I've willed, I'll do! . . .
The path to my fixed purpose is laid with iron rails, whereon my soul
is grooved to run." That he fails is no fault of his will; it carries him
as far as will can carry any man, almost literally into the jaws of
death. Like other tragic heroes he makes us realize the terror of the
gap between what the will can do and what reality can demand. Even
for Ahab, who "would strike the sun if it insulted" him, there is no
equation between the self and the real. But his effort to establish one
is awesome.

Ishmael's comically heroic effort is to abandon willfulness both of
the mind and of the spirit. It begins with his very first statement,
"Call me Ishmael," in which he discards his own name and invites
us to call him by the name of the Biblical outcast who, it was proph-
esied, would become the ancestor of a vast nation. He mocks his
own suicidal gloom and announces that he abominates "all honor-
able respectable toils, trials, and tribulations of every kind whatsoever." He goes to sea as a common sailor, cheerfully accepting the
indignities that are heaped on sailors by their officers. "Who ain't a
slave? Tell me that." And he no longer deludes himself that the
choices he made resulted from his "own unbiased freewill and discriminating judgment." He was simply responding to "an everlasting itch for things remote" and to the wonder that flooded his soul at
the image of "endless processions of the whale, and, midmost of
them all, one grand hooded phantom, like a snow hill in the air."

Yet abandoning willfulness is—as the good old willful saying has
it—easier said than done. Ishmael's implicit resolution is promptly
put to the test: he meets Queequeg and he hears Father Mapple's
sermon. He first responds to the "savage" harpooner as any good,
prideful, racist Christian should, with fear-filled rejection; but common sense, prompted by the lack of any other bed, tells him, "Better
sleep with a sober cannibal than a drunken Christian." "Never slept
better in my life," he reports. Nonetheless, the question of his relationship with Queequeg is still unsettled when he goes off the next day

to hear Father Mapple's sermon. The sermon is a superb piece of late Puritan eloquence, arguing that if we substitute God's will for our own we will know the delight, the "far, far upward, and inward delight," of standing forth "against the proud gods and commodores of this earth," "our own inexorable" selves, patriots only "to heaven." Characteristically, Ishmael makes not one single comment on Father Mapple's argument, but implicitly he rejects it. That night he reasons that it is the will of God that a good Christian, "born and bred in the bosom of the infallible Presbyterian Church," ought to worship before Queequeg's idol, Yojo; then he and Queequeg retire to the bed, in their heart's honeymoon, a cozy, loving pair. One can be sure that was not what Father Mapple had in mind.

Throughout these opening scenes with Queequeg, as later in the crucial scene of the squeezing of the sperm oil, Ishmael delights in using terms and images that are saturated with homosexual implications. This may or may not indicate that Melville himself was a latent, or repressed, or would-be homosexual, just as comparable imagery in *Leaves of Grass* may or may not tell us about the amorous life of Walt Whitman. Why worry about that? In *Moby-Dick,* as in *Leaves of Grass,* the significance of the imagery is that it mocks the fears of tight-willed heterosexuals. Unquestionably, one of the things that Ishmael learns is to relax his adult, well-trained, heterosexual will enough to accept and delight in a free-floating sensuality, in what Freudians would call "polymorphous perversity." This is made explicit in Ishmael's response to the vision of the "young Leviathan amours" in the center of the circle of whales in the chapter "The Grand Armada." "And thus, though surrounded by circle upon circle of consternations and affrights, did these inscrutable creatures at the centre freely and fearlessly indulge in all peaceful concernments; yea, serenely revelled in dalliance and delight. But even so, amid the tornadoed Atlantic of my being, do I myself still forever centrally disport in mute calm; and while ponderous planets of unwanting woe revolve round me, deep down and deep inland there I still bathe me in eternal mildness of joy."

Ishmael's response to whales and to Moby Dick in particular is

equal and opposite to Ahab's. One does not have to be a Freudian to
see that Ahab's fury is grounded in the fear that the whale that ampu-
tated his leg was attacking his masculinity. Ishmael, on the first day
of the chase, sees "a gentle joyousness" in Moby Dick and com-
pares him with "the white bull Jupiter swimming away with rav-
ished Europa clinging to his graceful horns." For a sailor who must
man an oar in a whaleboat to see gentle divinity in whales is as rare
and as heroic an action as for a wounded captain to pursue a single
whale, which he sees as the embodiment of all malignity, across the
oceans of the world.

Ishmael's intellectual response to reality is as free of will—of discipline and purpose—as his sensual response is. He loves to specu-
late about the world, to play with metaphors and to toy with analogies. He is as convinced as Ahab is that nature and the soul of man
are full of "linked analogies," but while Ahab is determined to
break through the mask, to *know* the true, final meaning of the analogies, Ishmael is happy to fool with them a while without the least
expectation of, or even desire for, certitude. His reveries on the
masthead are one good illustration of the way his mind functions; his
tongue-in-cheek interpretation of the symbolic significance of mat-
making is another. It is characteristic of Ishmael not to pursue a
speculation for very long, to drop a matter long before it yields a
coherent symbolic significance. His invocation of the sailor
Bulkington in chapter 23, "The Lee Shore," is a case in point; ear-
nest readers are often exasperated because after that one brief burst
of eloquence Ishmael never mentions Bulkington again. The same
readers are also exasperated by his refusal to organize all of his
cetological lore so that it will build toward some particular idea. But
Ishmael is not the man to fall "into Plato's honey head and sweetly
perish there"; nor will he trim the balance of his mind by hoisting
Locke's head on one side and Kant's on the other. His motto is the
opening sentence of chapter 82: "There are some enterprises in
which a careful disorderliness is the true method." Those are the
only enterprises he is interested in.

Just as he mocks masculinity and systematic thinking, he mocks the idea of free will and the dream of perfect independence (or self-reliance) which that idea generates. Ahab curses that "mortal inter-indebtedness" which makes him depend on the carpenter to carve a leg for him; Ishmael finds being tied to one end of the monkey-rope while Queequeg at the other end "cuts in" on the whale "a humorously perilous business." It does not bother him that his own individuality was merged with Queequeg's and "that his free will had received a mortal wound." He fully accepts the message he saw in Queequeg's eyes much earlier, when Queequeg rescued the country bumpkin who was swept overboard on the way to Nantucket: "It's a mutual, joint-stock world, in all meridians. We cannibals must help these Christians." Early and late, what Ishmael learns from Queequeg is to substitute acceptance for aggression. "No more my splintered heart and maddened hand were turned against the wolfish world. This soothing savage had redeemed it."

Such passive acceptance does not come easy, certainly not to Ishmael, probably not to any man. Proof of that is Ishmael's response to Ahab's "horrible oath." He joins in as fervently as any man on the *Pequod* and he does not wash himself of it quickly. However, proof is scarcely necessary; one does not need to *prove* that any man who voluntarily signed on for the bloody and perilous business of a whaling voyage in the middle of the nineteenth century had more than his fair share of aggressiveness.

An attempt to make a summary statement about Ishmael brings me back to my initial difficulty with terms. "Will" is roughly adequate to label the qualities of mind and spirit that Ishmael distrusts, but the best that can be said for "passivity" as a label for the qualities he trusts is that it is less misleading than any of the other words our language offers. Using it one must remember that Ishmael's passivity contains within it, however paradoxically, elements of fatalism, prankishness, and loving affirmation. He is hard to push—even Ahab's eloquence does not move him very far or for very long; Father Mapple's sermon does not budge him at all—and he refuses to pull, making no effort to change the minds of those around him or to control the next event. Whatever word or words we use to label the qualities that Ishmael embodies we should remember Melville's symbolic "definition" of them: they are the qualities that make it right for Ishmael to survive the catastrophe first by being thrown out of Ahab's boat by a blow from Moby Dick and then by floating on Queequeg's coffin, which is ornately carved with untranslatable hieroglyphs, until he is picked up by the *Rachel,* which is looking for someone else.

An essentially negative approach yields a somewhat clearer summary. Ishmael is not Ahab; he is Ahab's opposite in every respect. He is insistently mocking in his relationship with himself. He accepts as his peers those at the bottom of whatever hierarchy his society has devised; the only prince he associates himself with is a cannibal prince. He undercuts with ridicule every intellectually ambitious speculation he makes. And he is most careful to cut himself off from the conventional sources of masculine pride. Even in surviving Ishmael leaves himself with nothing to brag about; he would have us understand that it was luck, pure luck, that he survived while all the others were lost, as indeed it was. Whether Ishmael's odd kind of passivity is the cause or the effect of survivor's luck is an unanswerable question, for in the comic mode questions of cause and effect do not count for much. It is enough to know that here and elsewhere in comic art survivorship and such passivity are consistently associated with each other.

For another look at comedy's image of will, for a different type of passivity, I turn to Parson Adams. The differences between Adams and Ishmael are great, as great as the differences between Fielding's neoclassic imagination and Melville's romantic one. Ishmael is an outcast, by his own choice, from his society and from all of its institutions; Adams is so thoroughly embedded in his society that he cannot be imagined apart from it. He is, most emphatically, a priest of the established church and, almost as emphatically, a married man with several children. He is so thoroughly unrebellious that he does not even criticize his society, though he himself is frequently a victim of its arbitrary, class-structured institutions. He is also completely gregarious, loving ale, gossip, and the stories of other people's lives. Yet the basic similarity is there. Adams, too, is oddly passive. If Ishmael's passivity is like that of a log floating down a river, Adams's is like that of a ball bouncing down a hill. Adams seems much more energetic, for he collides with a number of people; but finally he exerts no more purposeful control over the sequence of events in his life than Ishmael does. He does not so much exert energy as obey the law of his own gravity.

Almost nothing that happens to Adams happens by his deliberate choice or as the result of any purposeful scheme of his. In fact, he is incapable of scheming, of organizing a sustained effort in order to serve a purpose. His one attempt to do so is ludicrous. As a grotesquely underpaid curate with a large family he is badly in need of money. He decides to get the money by taking a book-sized bundle of his sermons to London and selling them to a publish°r. There are two defects in his scheme: one is that he goes off without the sermons; the other, that even if he had them no publisher would buy them. When the defects are revealed to him at the time of his meeting with Joseph Andrews in an inn, he is undisturbed; he simply turns about with Joseph and heads for home with a new purpose, to marry Joseph and Fanny. His original moneymaking purpose is so weak that he cannot remember it long enough to act on it or even to regret its frustration. Indeed, his sense of money as a purpose is so weak that he cannot grasp the notion that people and events repeatedly conspire to teach him: that the way out of his troubles is to be deferential to powerful—that is, wealthy—people. In the society that Adams is embedded in that counts as a remarkable degree of purposelessness.

Adams shares in many of Ishmael's other qualities, too, though always with a difference. He, too, is egalitarian; Joseph and Fanny, both servants, are his equals, but so are Lady Booby and Peter Pounce. However, it is not a principled egalitarianism, as Ishmael's is; Adams just cannot seem to notice or to remember class distinctions. Adams is as free of vanity as Ishmael is, with one charming exception—he thinks very highly of his abilities as a teacher of classical languages and literature. He is also perfectly free of masculine pride. The outward sign of that state is his short-skirted cassock; the inward proof of it is his sexual innocence. He is practically the only man in the entire book who comes close to Fanny without lusting after her. He even gets in bed with her—by mistake of course—without noticing that she is there. Adams does have one of the conventional masculine attributes—he is a stout man in a fight—yet he is sweetly unaggressive. His numerous fights are simply the result of his unqualified willingness to come to the aid of injured innocence.

Adams is not the joker that Ishmael is; rather, he is the butt of every practical joker he meets. Nor is his intellect anything like Ishmael's; it is well disciplined with respect to classical learning and Christian thought, but in all other respects it is so undeveloped as to be almost childish. The result in the one case is a deliberate, sardonic unworldliness and in the other an absentminded unworldliness.

Adams, of course, is most separated from Ishmael by his sense of a religious obligation to serve others in accordance with the ideals and impulses of a charitable heart. In this he is much closer, by Fielding's avowed design, to Quixote whose obligation took the more bizarre form of serving as a knight-errant. In the grip of their obligations both Adams and Quixote are far more combative than Ishmael, yet they are essentially as unaggressive, as unthreatening as he is. Perhaps the comic moral is that the true hero, the comic hero, can possess a purpose and demonstrate valor if, and only if, his purpose strikes worldly people as insane (Adamsesque charity being nearly as insane as Quixotic knight-errantry) and his valor is perfectly selfless.

I am tempted to say that Adams, like Quixote, gives us comedy's image of passivity as seen from the right, but comedy is much too unruly to submit to schematization, especially when it is derived from bad political rhetoric. It would be better to say that Adams, like Quixote, gives us a strikingly clear, authentic vision of comic heroism, which is a passive rather than an assertive or willful heroism, as seen from the point of view of an artist who is thoroughly at home in his society. Certainly Fielding was at home wherever he went in eighteenth-century England, as Cervantes was in early seventeenth-century Spain, while Melville was always a transient in nineteenth-century America, no matter how long he stayed in one place.

The most finely accurate summaries are always those the artist gives us. For a summary symbolic statement about Adams one turns to chapter 14 of book 4, the bedroom farce scene. Briefly, Adams gets into the last of his many fights when he rushes out of his bedroom, without pausing to put his pants on, in order to rescue a damsel in distress in the next room. It is no damsel; it is Mrs. Slipslop. Nor is she in distress; rather, it is her supposed attacker, Beau Didapper, who is in distress. He had mistaken her room for Fanny's and had started to slip into her bed. Mrs. Slipslop realized the truth of the situation before he did, and since her reputation was in need of repair, she grabbed hold of him and yelled virtuously for help. In the dark, Adams mistakes the soft-skinned Beau for a woman and promptly begins punching Slipslop. By the time Lady Booby arrives with a light, Didapper has escaped and the fighting has stopped. To hide his nakedness from Lady Booby, Adams hops into the bed, where Slipslop is more than willing to make him welcome. However, Adams's virtue is unassailable, and he returns to his own room as soon as Lady Booby departs. But confused and impractical as always, Adams turns right instead of left and winds up in Fanny's room. A well-trained husband, Adams slips into the bed so quietly that he does not waken Fanny and prepares to sleep in his customary position, on the very edge of the bed. He does not discover the mistake until Joseph, who had an appointment to talk with Fanny at dawn, knocks at the door. " 'How!' said Joseph in a rage, 'hath he offered any rudeness to you?' She answered she could not accuse him of any more than villainously stealing to bed to her, which she thought rudeness sufficient, and what no man would do without a wicked intention.'' But Adams's intentions are never wicked, nor is his understanding ever very clear. He returns to his own room to dress for the day still half convinced that it was all the work of witches.

Throughout this scene Adams is ridiculous, but as Fielding sees it, being laughed at is the price a comic hero must pay for his heroism.

His reward is that he gets the prize others have been seeking furiously—Adams is the first man to get into Fanny's bed. Of course, he does not and never would use the prize as a prize. His triumph is that he officiates at the wedding of Fanny and Joseph. Like Ishmael's survival, Adams's triumph is the product of preposterous quantities of good luck; but one must observe that he never would have been in a position to benefit from luck if he had not been so stubborn in resisting every attempt to push or to lure him out of his fidelity to those loving hearts.

If Parson Adams is a rendition of the comically heroic qualities from the point of view of an imagination that is comfortably at home it its society, Heinrich Böll's Hans Schnier is a rendition of those qualities from the point of view of an imagination that is uncomfortably at home in its society. Just about every book that Böll has done—at least, just about every one that has been translated into English—deals in substantial part with his exasperation at the fate of being a German. The one possible exception is *Irish Journal,* a sketchbook of his experiences vacationing in Ireland in the fifties, but the exception is more apparent than real, for Ireland, especially the west of Ireland, serves throughout Böll's work as an example of a society that he would gladly have felt at home in if the fates had been kinder. However, he is not Irish, he is German. He is stuck with that fate; he cannot emigrate from it, for he would carry Germany with him just as surely as Nabokov carried Russia with him throughout all the years of his enforced emigration. Most American writers could sympathize with Böll's sense of his fate because it is so much like their own sense of their similar fate. Faulkner offers the most exact parallel; as he was stuck in and with the American South, Böll is stuck in and with the German Rhineland.

Hans Schnier is a representative Böllian hero—that is, he is a Rhinelander who has rejected everything his society expected him to accept without ever rebelling against it. "What kind of a man are you?" his brother Leo asks in exasperation. "I am a clown," he replies, "and I collect moments." Leo, who is said "to have a future" as a Catholic theologian, is a realist; but Hans is not an -*ist* of any kind, not even a momentist, for the -*ist* ending implies some sort of abstract conviction and Hans has none. He is as free from abstractions as it is possible for a modern man to be. Abstractions arise from a sense of history, from a perception that moments and the events that take place in them are not discrete but are fused together by underlying causes or meanings. Hans has no sense of history. He collects moments, each of which is too miraculous to submit to generalization, and does honor to them with his art. (Americans would call that art pantomime rather than clowning, for it resembles the work of Marcel Marceau and has nothing to do with circuses.)

Because the abstract ideas that fuel so much social behavior—communism and capitalism, Catholicism and Protestantism, race and nation, prestige and respectability—simply do not exist for the clown, he does not have to rebel against them. To put it another way, because the abstractions do not exist for him, they do not arouse in him the emotions—fear, greed, pride, and envy—that generate aggression in most of us. Consequently, he is remarkably free of aggressiveness. He is, even in the most common senses of the word, a passive hero. He could also be called a saintly hero, for his devotion to the moment frees him from most of the deadly sins, even lust. Since he has experienced "the thing that men do with women" only with Marie, and since he knows that was a miraculous and exceedingly complex experience, he is practically incapable of generalizing desire enough to feel lust. All of the talk of churchmen about "the desires of the flesh" strikes him as dangerous, oversimplified nonsense. Ironically, the marriage of this hopelessly monogamous man to his Marie, which was never a legal marriage because he resisted a state involvement in their relationship and because he refused to put into writing his willingness to raise in the Catholic church any children they might have, is broken by a group of Catholic intellectuals who save Marie from "a life of sin" by persuading her to leave Hans and to marry, in ceremonies sanctioned by both church and state, a "good" (and intellectual) Catholic.

A man for whom abstractions scarcely exist is bound to get into all sorts of trouble, perhaps especially in Germany. As a child during the war, Hans could not make any sense out of the demand that he be a "good German," and the results are nearly fatal. As an adult he still does not know how to be a good German of either the Western or the Eastern variety. He holds all of West Germany's political parties in contempt, especially for their terror of any idea that can be even remotely connected with communism; yet when he goes to East Germany to perform, he winds up in disgrace because he flatly refuses to serve propaganda with his art. (Specifically, Hans refuses to do his "turn" on boards of directors on the ground that it seems "pretty low" to poke fun at them in a country that does not have boards of directors, and his hosts are not interested in having him work up a new routine, "The Party Conference Elects its Presidium.") His only political position is that he "likes the kind to which he belongs—people." Naturally, that does not satisfy anyone.

As "a brown-coal Schnier"—as a member of a family that for seventy years has owned a sizable block of shares in a company that mines brown coal—Hans ought to have a properly subtle sense of and a conservative regard for class distinctions, but if they register at all with him, his response is "wrong." He dislikes upper middle-class manners as he has seen them operate in his family; he likes the coarseness and warmth he has observed in working-class families; and he detests middle-class intellectualism, especially when it is applied to theology and art. His Marie is the daughter of a man who has "come down in the world" because his political and religious beliefs are always wrong and who is barely surviving with a small stationery shop that also sells candy to school children; and Hans warmly supported the efforts of a working-class boy to court his sister, Henrietta.

Hans is neither a Catholic, like his brother the seminarian, nor a Protestant, like the rest of the Schniers; he is not even an atheist. He does like to sing the Litany of Loreto, especially while soaking in a hot tub after a performance, and he admires the "only four Catholics in the world: Pope John, Alec Guinness, Marie, and Gregory, an old Negro boxer who had once nearly become world champion and who is now eking out a meagre living as a strong man in vaudeville."

Hans is nearly destroyed by the forces of abstraction, as embodied in such "realistic" people as the head of the Christian Educational Society, who not only cheats him out of most of his fee after a bad performance but works zealously to destroy his professional reputation, the circle of Catholic intellectuals who break up his marriage, his father, who cannot bring himself to break his allegiance to "abstract money" long enough to be generous to him when he badly needs help, and his mother. Each of the four pushes him toward a form of despair.

It is relatively easy for Hans to resist the professional despair that the Christian educator is so maliciously, and thriftily, trying to engender. He is, after all, a true clown who has done good work in the past and can do it again in the future, and he has resigned himself to the fact that agents and entrepreneurs will always take what advantage they can of artists. "An artist simply cannot help doing what he does . . . ; an artist is like a woman who can do nothing but love, and who succumbs to every stray male jackass." His father, who is so much the very model of a modern German businessman that he frequently appears on television to express the business point of view, is naturally a more difficult problem. But Hans can reconcile himself to his father despite his managerial manners and his compulsive loyalty to "money in the abstract" because he had once been human enough to save three women from a pompous Nazi colonel who wanted to execute them as spies and saboteurs for going behind the American lines to get bread from a relative's bakery, and because he remained human enough to need some warmth in his life, keeping a sweet, circumspect, empty-headed opera singer as a mistress. His father, he finally realizes, is not a realist.

His mother is a much more depressing burden for Hans, for she is a stupid, stingy, vain, and ruthlessly proper woman. As a child, he never had quite enough to eat, not even of potatoes, partly because she could not resist an opportunity to save a penny, and partly because she was anxious to keep her figure slim. Far worse, because she wanted to be known as a patriot, in February 1945 she sent his sixteen-year-old sister, Henrietta, to an anti-aircraft battery where she could do her bit "to drive the Jewish Yankees from our sacred

German soil.'' The news of Henrietta's death in battle touched off Hans's only outburst of aggressive behavior: he raced through the house grabbing everything of hers he could lay hands on, pitched it through the window, and set fire to the whole pile. Years later, Hans is still aching with grief over the slaughter of that innocent; his mother is as fashionably patriotic as ever, now as a member of the Executive Committee of the Societies for the Reconciliation of Racial Differences (and carefully billing the committee for all of her expenses). Needless to say, though she is a patroness of the respectable arts, she does not consider clowning an art and does not use any of her six-figure bank account to help Hans. But his art, his clown's dedication to ''moments,'' leads him to a way of saving himself from despair over her; remembering that he once watched her ''go secretly into her storeroom in the basement, cut herself a thick slice of ham and eat it down there, standing, with her fingers, hurriedly,'' he realizes that she, too, is of that kind to which he belongs: people. Out of kindness he determines to keep her secret; it ''will rest under a marble slab in the Schnier vault.''

As for the despair that the Catholic intellectuals have so piously heaped upon him by ''seducing'' Marie, Hans finally refuses the burden. He will clown his way to freedom, and he is sure that Marie will come with him.

The course of *The Clown,* like the course of Ishmael's story and like the course of *Joseph Andrews,* is the course of comedy. Hans Schnier is driven lower and lower by the forces of abstraction, by ''realistic'' powers; he is brought to the very edge of despair by his loyalty to the moment and to his art, by his rejection of all abstract considerations, by his ''passivity.'' Then, he is saved from self-pity and suicide by the very qualities that nearly destroyed him. At that rock bottom, when he paints his face all white so that ''he looks like a corpse playing a corpse,'' he rediscovers the strength of his art and the validity of his dedication to moments; he starts to rise. Like Ishmael and Parson Adams, Hans survives. At the very end, he sits on the steps at the railway station in white face and jumper, playing his guitar, singing a song he has made up about ''poor Pope John,'' catching coins in his cup, and waiting for Marie to come in on the train from Rome, confident that she will return to him.

These three very different heroes from three very different novels written in three different countries and in three different centuries act out for us the passivity that is in some degree characteristic of all comic heroes and which I take to be the crucial element in comedy's image of that portion of the self which deals with controlling and organizing behavior. The central point is that none of them solves his problems by taking purposeful action; each waits for something to happen that will bring about a solution. Ishmael does not resolve to break his allegiance to Ahab; he simply washes "his hand and heart" of that "horrible oath" while squeezing the sperm oil. Nor does he stand up for his principles by rebelling against Ahab's orders; he waits to be knocked out of the boat by the whale and waits again, on Queequeg's coffin, to be picked up by "the devious cruising *Rachel.*" Adams does not resolve the confusions that block Joseph's marriage to Fanny any more than he finds a way to solve his own economic problems; he just stands ready—obstinately so—to perform the ceremony at the earliest proper opportunity. Hans Schnier's only purposeful act is to put on the costume of his art and go to the railroad station to wait for Marie to come back to him; through most of *The Clown* he is in his apartment, drinking, remembering, and talking on the telephone, but not planning or taking any purposeful action.

One sees the same quality in the other comic heroes I have discussed in earlier chapters. Quixote crystallizes it in his gesture of dropping the reins to let Rocinante decide the direction they will take. Huck approaches purposefulness with his famous "All right, then, I'll *go* to hell," but it turns out that he lets Tom lead the action, just as earlier he had followed his decision to flee with Jim by getting on a raft to float to wherever the river would take them, even when it took them past the Ohio and deep into the slave states. In *The Horse's Mouth* Gulley Jimson's passivity is shown on two levels, as he deals with his essentially superficial problem of getting money and his fundamental problem of grasping the images he needs for

"The Creation." His efforts to get money are ridiculously incompetent—a mixture of petty thievery and transparent confidence games—until Nosy Barbon comes in puffing with indignation over the poor copy he has seen an art student making of one of Gulley's early paintings of Sara Monday which is now hanging in the Tate; Gulley finally gets the brilliant idea of faking a preliminary study for it which he can sell for a sizable amount of money because he can give it "an irrefutable pedigree." Even then, Gulley half botches the job; in a hurry to dry the study, he puts it in an oven and raises blisters on "poor Sara's behind." And in the truly important matter of "The Creation" Gulley shows that an artist cannot command the lightning of inspiration any more than a joke-maker can; despite all of his hard work, he must wait for the accident of a night in the woods to supply him with the crucial central image.

Any quick skim over comic literature would turn up plenty of other examples of heroes who steadfastly drift into their crucial actions, preferring to trust in luck rather than in their own will. Leopold Bloom, who wanders almost aimlessly around Dublin, is a fine, clear example; Berger's Jack Crabb (in *Little Big Man*), who bumps back and forth between Indian and white cultures, is another. So is Odysseus, who perhaps set the pattern by taking ten years to return to Ithaca. True, he finally comes to terrifying action in the slaughter of the suitors, but he depends on the Phaiakians to bring him to Ithaca and on Pallas Athene to prompt and assist in his decisive action. Falstaff burlesques all noble, resolute behavior, and the good soldier Švejk, like Heller's Yossarian, makes a farce of military honor. And—to cite one last, very different example—James's "ambassador," Lambert Strether, achieves his heroic stature first by refusing to do anything to get Chad out of Paris and finally by taking a trip into the country, choosing his destination perfectly at random and discovering there the truth which sets him free from Woollett, Massachusetts.

A similar distrust of willful, rationally purposeful action and a similar capacity for waiting until somebody or something precipitates the crucial action is expressed through comic heroines, too. But the similarity is more real than apparent because a heroine is like the Frenchman that Jim argues about with Huck—she does not *talk* like a man. A feminine expression of an image is likely to seem as different from a masculine expression as ''How are you?'' from ''Comment allez-vous?'' And, of course, it is a lot easier to say some things in one language than in another, which is why the French have borrowed ''le weekend'' from us and we have filched ''rapport'' from them.

For example, take the common comic business of deriding ideals of efficiency. It is relatively simple to do it through a masculine character as Cary does through Gulley Jimson with his elaborate schemes for making some money, or as Amis does through Jim Dixon in *Lucky Jim.* Jim loathes and fears all of the people around him who know how to forge ahead in the academic world; he gets drunk when he has to visit his department head's home or deliver a public lecture, and he strikes back at all of them mostly by making horrible faces before his mirror. The reader begins by laughing at Jim but ends (if he is a sympathetic reader) by seeing his ineptitude as a criticism of the stuffy academic world and as a sign of his superiority to it. That is, because Jim is a man his ineptitude can be seen as more or less deliberately chosen and as meaningful. If a writer were to try to handle the same theme in the same way through a female character, the odds are that she would be seen as yet another feather-brained woman for a reader to condescend to.

The comic heroine in whom it is easiest to see similarity to Ishmael, Parson Adams, and Hans Schnier is Cary's Sara Monday, more as she is seen in her own narrative, *Herself Surprised,* than in the other two books of the trilogy, *To Be a Pilgrim* and *The Horse's Mouth.* Like the comic heroes, she is a drifter and improvisor of a most durable sort. She begins as a cook in the household of an elderly widow, Mrs. Monday. She is perfectly content with that position and that status, but the widow's son, Matt, a shy, awkward, homely forty-year-old bachelor, pesters her into marrying him. At least that is her first version of what happened; later on she is forced to admit that she might have led him on a bit, even though she cer-

tainly did not intend to. As Mrs. Monday, she is again perfectly
content with her position and status. Though the status bothers her at
first, she solves that problem by not changing her habits and attitudes,
and society in their town does come to accept her as she is, garish
clothes and all. It helps that she made a "conquest" of the leading
gentleman of the area, Mr. Hickson, by flirting with him out-
rageously, but since she did it for Matt's sake, and since nothing
really came of it, that is all right. When she does the same thing, four
children and a number of years later, with an artist Hickson is pro-
moting, Gulley Jimson, quite a lot comes of it. There is no need to
get into a summary of all of *Herself Surprised* and much of *The
Horse's Mouth;* it is sufficient to say that Sara drifts up and down in
society and in and out of a succession of liaisons, none of which ever
quite becomes a legal marriage.

Through it all Sara remains Sara. Tommy Wilcher, her employer
at Tolbrook who takes to warming himself in her bed and who is
finally most anxious to marry her, sees her as "saved," as "one of
those people to whom faith is so natural that they don't know how
they have it." Gulley sees her and paints her as "the real old original
fireship," as "the everlasting Eve." The judge who sentences her to
prison at the beginning of *Herself Surprised*—for stealing things
from Wilcher—sees her as "another unhappy example of that laxity
and contempt for all religious principle and social obligation which
threatens to undermine the whole fabric of our civilization." But
Sara, who pays no attention to why she is doing what she is doing or
how it will look to others, has no idea of what she is, she simply is.

Thus, she fits in several categories, and in none; she is simultaneously amorphous and unchanging. That is, she is very much like
the comic heroes I have discussed, possessing fully and plainly the
odd passivity that comedy admires and trusts. Yet there is an important difference: her avoidance of purpose and aggression is effortless;
theirs involves some degree of strategy or exception. For a reasonably clear explanation, I must shift to the terms *intuition* and *concept*
that Cary works with in *Art and Reality*.

Cary argues that as children we perceive reality intuitively, directly, without help or hindrance from any concept, but as we grow older our experience practically forces us to develop concepts, which become, once they are fully established, a kind of crust over reality. The lively, individual bundle of feathers that fascinates and delights us as children becomes, quickly enough, just another sparrow to be ignored. Cary does not sentimentalize about the deadening effects of concepts in the manner of recent theorists of education, for he knows that they are both inevitable and necessary. People who do not develop concepts about the dangers of fires, knives, and automobiles are not likely to live long, and people who do not possess skill in working with concepts are liable to be useless to themselves and others for all sorts of important purposes. Yet Cary recognizes the danger: that people can become the prisoners of their concepts, blocked from any effective contact with living reality. The function of art, he thinks, is to help us to avert that danger, for art breaks through the conceptual crust that overlies our ordinary experience and gives us, at least in our imaginations, direct intuitive perception of our world. Gulley Jimson is his portrait of the artist as an old man—that is, one who has mastered all of the traditional skills of painting but has finally broken free of them to do his own distinctive work. "Look at me," he says to Lady Beeder, who has been showing him some of her nice, well-trained watercolors. "One of the cleverest painters who ever lived. . . . If I hadn't been lucky I might have spent the rest of my life doing conjuring tricks to please the millionaires, and the professors. But I escaped. . . . Why, your ladyship, a lot of my recent stuff is not much better, technically, than any young lady can do after six lessons at a good school. Heavy-handed, stupid-looking daubery. Only difference is that it's about something—it's an experience."

But Cary knows that there are exceptions to all generalizations, even his own. Sara Monday is one of his great exceptions. She has relatively little education and she is not in any formal sense an artist. Yet she is free to live her own life in her own way and to be a blessing to others, at least to others who are not the captives of concepts. The judge who sentences her to prison and Wilcher's furiously

respectable niece, Blanche, who sicked the police on her, are captives; and her freedom baffles and enrages them. Sara's gift is to feel
accurately about her world without ever thinking about it. Or to put it
another way, she uses words smoothly, even glibly sometimes, without ever thinking about their meanings; she knows their colors and
tones without paying attention to their concepts. Thus, Sara airily
dismisses Hickson's jealous complaint, made when she was still
married to Matt Monday, that she was seeing too much of Jimson
and posing for him in the nude: "Which was false, and what was
worse, unfriendly." Strictly speaking, Sara is wrong. She had in
carnal fact been "seeing too much of Jimson" and she had certainly
posed for him without any clothing on. But essentially she is right.
Her actions did not mean what Hickson judged them to mean and his
complaint was most certainly unfriendly. Hickson wanted and meant
to have a nice genteel *ménage à trois;* Sara, who was untroubled by
gentility and unconcerned with numbers, simply was willing to en-
large the *ménage* that she had created around Matt.

Because concepts have no real meaning for Sara, her behavior is
not controlled by them. She simply acts out the realities that others
attempt to generalize with conceptual terms, such as *wife, mother,
servant, thief,* but it is impossible to describe accurately or even to
understand her behavior in those terms. She is a "bad" wife to Matt
because she is "unfaithful" to him with Gulley, but whatever force
and vitality came into his life came through his relationship with
Sara. He had been a timid, nervous, henpecked son and brother
until he was forty; then he married her and began to count for something in his home and his community. In the old-fashioned phrase,
she was the making of him, which is the classic work of a good wife.
She was an equally good wife later to Tommy Wilcher, Fred, and
Byles, though she did not marry any of them. With Gulley she was a
different (though similarly unofficial) kind of wife, for there was no
possibility of domesticating him. "Life with Sara," he says in *The
Horse's Mouth,* "was all on the diplomatic scale, between the grand
contracting parties. Sometimes we were noble allies and carried on
the war together, sometimes we were enemies; but you were always

yourself and Sara was always herself, and making love to Sara was a stormy joy, thunder and lightning. There was an exchange of powers, a flash and a bang; Jupiter and the cloud. You gave something and you took something.''

I doubt that any dealer in used concepts would ever call Sara ''a wifely woman.'' Similarly, he could not call her ''motherly.'' She may have been great at nurturing children, whether they were hers or not, but she lost all track of them after they left the nest, and she never subsided into motherliness. ''Servant'' will not do, because she is too independent and too insensitive about delicate matters of status. And though she does commit various illegalities with odds and ends of Wilcher's property, it is ridiculous to call her a thief. This is one thing Sara does *understand* and her comment on what came out at her trial is fully justified: ''It is very hard to get truth into evidence, as I think it is hard enough to get it in life, about human people, or even yourself.''

The only generalization that will fit Sara is symbolic rather than conceptual: she is a descendant of the Wife of Bath. She is not as bawdy as Chaucer's great original nor is she as talkative, but she shares in her vitality, her bland disregard for concepts, priestly and otherwise, and her capacity for reaching out to others in such a way that it is impossible to tell whether she is being selfish or generous. Such a woman is too free of ego to be called egotistical but so aware of her small comforts and sensual pleasures and so stubbornly resistant to control that one is sorely tempted to damn her as self-centered. But she is not. Or if she is, it is a notably inclusive self that she is centered on, a self that is as roomy and as unpretentious as an old-fashioned, slightly seedy seaside hotel.

There are plenty of other descendants of the Wife of Bath scattered throughout comic literature. Mostly they are figures in the background, women a hero comes to or upon for aid and comfort before he takes up his burdens again; too often, of course, they are reduced to that cliché of second-rate imaginations, the whore with a heart of gold. Of the extended characterizations of this type of heroine the best known, and the best, are DeFoe's Moll Flanders and Joyce's

Molly Bloom. Molly speaks for all of them, Sara Monday most defi-
nitely included: "And I thought as well him as another and then I
asked him with my eyes to ask again yes and then he asked me would
I yes to say yes my mountain flower and first I put my arms around
him yes and drew him down to me so he could feel my breasts all
perfume yes and his heart was going like mad and yes I said yes I
will Yes." The key words, please note, are *and* and *yes*.

Those may be the key words for all who possess, or are possessed
by, the comic vision, though many, like William Congreve's
Millamant, speak them only in a wittily disguised fashion: "These
articles subscribed, if I continue to endure you a little longer, I may
by degrees dwindle into a wife." The descendants of the Wife of
Bath seem to be incapable of disguise, perhaps because like Sara
Monday they are perpetually surprised by themselves, surprised to
discover what they have said and done, surprised to discover how
others have seen them, and perpetually resolving to "keep a more
watchful eye, next time, on my flesh, now that I know it better." But
there is another, much larger class of comic heroines to whom disguise is as natural as breathing. They are, to offer a parallel category,
descendants of Pallas Athene, the gray-eyed goddess who was mistress of all feigning. Her scene with Odysseus upon the beach at
Ithaka is crucial. She comes to him in disguise, naturally. When he
responds to her questions with a detailed, plausible, wholly false
story of who he is and what he is doing, she sheds her disguise,
revealing herself in all her "tall beauty," and for once expresses
directly her admiration for a man who is "so civilized, so intelligent,
so self-possessed" (E. V. Rieu's translation) that he will, even on
the morning he has achieved a goal he has sought for ten years,
invent and play "a part as though it were his own tough skin"
(Robert Fitzgerald's translation). The descendants of Pallas Athene
are those comic heroines who know that in a hard, dangerous world
mortals must use their wits to protect and preserve themselves and
those they love, and who have the wit to do it. Words are their
weapons and they use them brilliantly. Chief among them are
Rosalind, Célimène, Millamant, and Elizabeth Bennet, though one

can find such heroines in nearly all novels and plays that are concerned with reconciling the inevitable conflict between self and society.

In Rosalind the major qualities of this type of heroine are plain to see. Her disguise is both physical and psychological. She dresses and swaggers like a man to fool a hostile world, and she plays and talks like a man to teach her lover to be less foolish. Yet she never gets so carried away by her role, as poor players do, as to forget the difference between her true self and her assumed self. Indeed, one feels that the more she plays the masculine part of Ganymede, the more accurately she sees, and the more fully she accepts the needs and limitations of her feminine self. Moreover, she uses words superbly on all occasions, whether she is practicing wordplay with Celia, shutting off Touchstone's mockery of Orlando's bad poetry, dismissing Jaques's fashionable melancholia, giving Orlando instruction on the nature of women, characterizing the sudden love between Celia and Oliver, or confessing to Celia ''how many fathom deep'' she is in love. Even when she is momentarily at a loss for words, after fainting at the news of Orlando's wounding by a lion, her language is precisely controlled: ''I would that I were at home.'' That says exactly what she feels without revealing anything she needs to keep concealed.

The same qualities are reasonably plain in both Célimène and Millamant. Neither dons a literal disguise (Millamant scorns the notion that she might wear a mask to a play), yet both do a lovely job of misleading the world by pretending to be social butterflies. Millamant's disguise is described by two lines of Mirabell's: the first, announcing her arrival in act 2 of *The Way of the World*, ''Here she comes, i'faith, full sail, with her fan spread and her streamers out, and a shoal of fools for tenders''; the second, commenting on her swift departure at the end of that scene, ''Think of you! To think of a whirlwind, though 'twere in a whirlwind, were a case of more steady contemplation.'' Molière does not supply anywhere in *The Misanthrope* such a quotable description of Célimène's disguise, but it is beautifully dramatized in the scene (2.5) in which she regales

her fashionable suitors and disgusts Alceste with a virtuoso performance as a gossip. Certainly both Millamant and Célimène can play
dazzlingly with words. One example from each is sufficient: Millamant's speech about how she is "persecuted" with letters from
would-be lovers that culminates in her comment that at least the ones
in verse were good for pinning up her hair—"I never pin up my hair
with prose. I fancy one's hair would not curl if it were pinned up
with prose" (act 2). And Célimène's comment (2.5) on Alceste's
belief that a true lover would shun flattery and candidly correct his
beloved's faults:

> If all hearts beat according to your measure,
> The dawn of love would be the end of pleasure;
> And love would find its perfect consummation
> In ecstasies of rage and reprobation.
>   (Richard Wilbur's translation)

Few people who can read English would quarrel with an assertion
that Elizabeth Bennet uses words exceedingly well. It appears harder
to argue that she shares with the other descendants of Pallas Athene a
gift for disguise, for she neither dresses as a man nor pretends to be a
social butterfly. Yet there is something very much like a gift for
disguise in the mockery with which she comments on Darcy's first
haughty estimate of her as "tolerable, but not handsome enough to
tempt" him, and in the wittiness with which she shuts off her mother's humiliatingly foolish chatter by holding forth on "the efficacy of
poetry in driving away love." Similarly her self-control in her scenes
with Lady Catherine at Rosings and at Longbourn serve to shield, if
not disguise, her feelings. Elizabeth's character, unlike Lady
Catherine's, will never be "celebrated for its sincerity and frankness." Indeed, it is an affecting bit of comedy when she becomes so
flustered when Darcy brings his sister and Bingley to call on her and
the Gardiners that she does not know how to deal with, let alone
conceal, her feelings.

Unlike the other heroines, Elizabeth comes close to being caught
inside the mask she has chosen to wear. The second half of *Pride and*

Prejudice could be described as a portrayal of her increasing mastery of that mask, the scene of her embarrassment at the inn in Lambton being the failure that makes it possible for mastery to develop. Looking at the second half this way, her scene with Lady Catherine is a sort of final examination of her skill in handling the mask confidently and exactly, and the closing scenes—with Darcy, with Jane, and, in a letter, with her Aunt Gardiner—are a demonstration of completely matured mastery. With Darcy, she is open but playful, yet sensible enough to remember that "he had yet to learn to be laught at." With Jane, who is anxious to know how long she has loved Darcy, she both reveals and protects emotional truth by replying, "I believe I must date it from my first seeing his beautiful grounds at Pemberley." And in her letter to Aunt Gardiner, she manages to be open and warm without being girlish and effusive: "I am the happiest creature in the world. Perhaps other people have said so before, but not one with such justice. I am happier even than Jane; she only smiles, I laugh."

Of course, there are sentimentalists who cannot see much to Millamant but the disguise she wears. The world of *The Way of the World* is too cold a place for them, and they cannot believe that a woman of *real* feeling would conduct herself with all the playful artifice that Millamant displays in the contract scene. More numerous and much more articulate are the Rousseauistic romantics who are so anxious to see Alceste as an image of heroic sincerity that they cannot perceive Célimène as anything but the vain, shallow worldling she pretends to be. There is no simple, direct evidence of any emotional depth to her, nothing equivalent to Mrs. Fainall's testimony that Millamant is indeed far gone in love for Mirabell. Molière is much too austere a dramatist to *tell* you anything; he simply shows you a young woman who is astonishingly good at playing all the little games an aristocratic society delights in and who is loved by an astonishingly surly man who is revolted by the hypocrisy and insincerity which flourish in that society. Even while she is flirting with assorted marquesses, she assures him that he is the one she truly loves. That is not good enough for him; he wants her entirely to himself. Catching her at a moment of minor social disgrace (one of her virtuoso performances has come back to embarrass her), he offers to marry her on the condition that she join him in flying to some "solitary place" where they can "forget the human race." She agrees to marriage but not to hermitage. Indignant—"Must you have me, and all the world beside?"—Alceste stomps off to find a pure and noble solitude, leaving Célimène still enmeshed in an impure, ignoble, but amusing world. Which, of course, is just where she wants to be. Alceste is a fool. He is by far the most intelligent man in the drama, which is apparently why Célimène loves him, but a fool nonetheless. He has condemned Célimène for her greatest gift: "I see dear lady, that you could make a case / For putting up with the whole human race." Precisely. She is a mediator, so gifted a one that she could, if he would let her, mediate between Alceste and their society. She knows something that Alceste is too arrogant to understand—that an individual needs the whole human race more than the race needs any given individual. Where Alceste is going there will be no fops and sonneteers, but neither will there be any Célimènes. Where Célimène is, there will be more, and better, Alcestes. If there are not any, she will make one. That is what the descendants of Pallas Athene do; that is their comically heroic purpose. Shaw explains that clearly—perhaps a little too clearly—in *Man and Superman*. In the body of the play Ann Whitefield pursues and captures Jack Tanner and in the dream scene Dona Ana follows Don Juan from hell to heaven; both are determined to create the superman.

Certainly that is what Rosalind does in *As You Like It*—she makes a better Orlando. Or, because that is an old-fashioned, easily misunderstood way of putting it, she teaches him to bring his intelligence to bear on his emotions. Or, because that is an excessively simple, trite way of putting it, she teaches him to view her and her relationship with him realistically rather than idealistically and thereby to understand the depth and power of their interdependence. Or, because that is not quite an adequate way of putting it either, she teaches him to use words accurately rather than tritely. Well, that is not it, either. The Shakespearean truth is that Rosalind is no butterfly to be pinned to a display board with a few general terms.

Recapitulation, as simple as possible, will work better. Rosalind meets Orlando and promptly falls many fathoms deep in love with him. Apparently, she is responding to the strength and courage he displays in his match with the dangerous professional wrestler, and to the sweetness and simplicity of character that he reveals in a few short speeches. Probably she is also responding to his forlornness, which is congruent with her own. Each of them badly needs somebody with the qualities the other has: she needs his strength and courage in battle for protection in a violent world; he needs her wit and perspicacity for protection in a treacherous society. But before she will give herself to him—more accurately, before she will let them join together—she disguises herself as a man and puts him through a mock courtship; in this process they both learn much. Orlando learns not to disgrace himself and her by littering the forest of Arden with bad, lovesick verses; more fundamentally, he learns to desire a woman for what she is, complex and difficult as she may be, not for some silly, sentimental notion of what she might or ought to be. Having to dissemble, Rosalind learns how powerful and how important her love for Orlando is to her; also, her experience as an imitation man teaches her to value the genuine article even more. The advice she gives to Phebe is heartfelt: "Down on your knees, and thank heaven, fasting, for a good man's love." And the comment she makes about Celia and Oliver, which is disturbing to delicate sensibilities, also arises out of self-knowledge: "They are in the very wrath of love and they will together; clubs cannot part them." At the end, having presided over or at least condoned the various courtships, Rosalind gives final responsibility to Hymen, the god of marriage and therefore "god of every town." Hand in hand, she and Orlando join the circle of those who are to marry and thereby to recreate society.

Playful and witty, Rosalind is as opposite to a hero of tragedy or of melodrama as any hero of comedy, whether it be Ishmael, Parson

Adams, Hans Schnier, Don Quixote, or Huck Finn. So, too, are Célimène, Millamant, and Elizabeth Bennet. All are in their very feminine ways models of the comic virtue I have called passivity (for lack of a better word). They do not attempt to impose their wills on the world, but they will not let the world impose its will on them. Rosalind is representative: she does nothing to effect the revolution that is necessary to release her and those she loves from exile in the forest of Arden, but when release comes she is ready to take the greatest possible advantage of it.

To use Lynch's term again, Rosalind and these other heroines embody the analogical intelligence that comedy celebrates. That is why it is so difficult to make generalizations about what Rosalind is or what she does. Her delight in love is analogical rather than analytical. She insists to Orlando that his Rosalind can be and will be this way, that way, and the other way, yet always Rosalind, just as she demonstrates to us that she is fully Rosalind while being Ganymede. Nothing that she says or does permits us to make categorical, classifying statements about the ideal lover; but she keeps discovering and refining the lover in a wide variety of people. A univocal intelligence focuses on and seeks to abstract or define the sameness that it discovers in a number of separate cases; an analogical intelligence like Rosalind's savors all the different forms in which a sameness can be discovered. At the play's end, Rosalind and Orlando, Celia and Charles, Phebe and Silvius, and Audrey and Touchstone are all married lovers yet each couple is different. Critics of a univocal turn of mind often object to the presence of Touchstone in the charming nuptial group, but there he is and there he belongs. "A poor virgin, sir, an ill-favored thing, sir, but mine own" is simply a harsh, sardonic—that is, masculine—refraction of Rosalind's mockery of sentimental idealism about love.

Rosalind's achievement is that she combines social realism with romantic ardor without blurring or weakening either; it is grounded in unblinking self-knowledge. She knows that she is both intelligent and ardent, and she insists on being both at once. In the same way, she knows that she is both a woman—a unit of the race—and an individual, both a social being who is incomplete without others and a self whose private imperative must be respected. Thus, she is both remarkably independent and wholly dependent, first on Orlando and ultimately on Hymen, the "god of every town." In their very different circumstances and ways, Millamant, Célimène, and Elizabeth Bennet display the same kind of duality, though Célimène does not enjoy the triumph of a union with her beloved.

Some people question whether this duality deserves to be called heroic; I do not. I have long since accepted Henry James's argument in "The Art of Fiction" that "for a Bostonian nymph to reject an English duke is an adventure only less stirring . . . than for an English duke to be rejected by a Bostonian nymph." Of course, people with imaginations that I would deride as essentially military cannot share James's sense of an adventure and cannot grant heroism even to the heroes of comedy, except perhaps to Odysseus, and then they are unwilling to see the *Odyssey* as a comedy. Comic heroes like Yossarian and the good soldier Švejk are not given to defending the pass against hordes of invaders. But even some people who accept the heroism of comic heroes deny the heroism of comic heroines, essentially on the ground that only those who maintain some sort of open dissent from society's values are worthy of the special admiration we accord to the heroic. In this view, as expressed by Robert M. Torrance in *The Comic Hero* (p. ix), since women have not, at least until very recently, been permitted the transgressions against society that we have condoned in men, they have been constrained to adopt gentler, unheroic modes of remonstrance. Maybe, but that seems to me suspiciously like a sophisticated form of the naive view that heroism is revealed only in combat. Comedy has as much to do with reconciliation as with dissent, and certainly the comic heroines whom I have labeled the descendants of Pallas Athene demonstrate the great comic virtues of courage and gaiety as fully as any heroes do. Elizabeth Bennet is a strong case.

Elizabeth's courage is as vivid as that of any beribboned soldier and much rarer, I think. The annals of war are full of accounts of men who have had the courage to charge the cannon's mouth; the annals of peace do not tell of so many people who have had the courage to dismiss great wealth as Elizabeth does when she rejects Darcy's first offer of marriage. Indeed, painfully few of us are up to saying no—bluntly and firmly—to anything like the equivalent of Darcy's ten thousand a year. True, he offered it in a graceless way, but the gracelessness of offers of money have rarely impeded the eagerness of acceptances. And Elizabeth says no with her back to the wall: as the daughter of an improvident gentleman whose estate is entailed, she *must* either marry a man of means or submit to a hideously circumscribed life on the fringe of polite society. Yet she says it and means it, as much as she meant her rejection of Mr. Collins's far less tempting offer, which was too much for her friend Charlotte Lucas to reject, or as much as she meant her decision to reject the blandishments of Wickham, which were too tempting to her sister Lydia. It takes courage for her to stand up to Darcy as she does, and then it takes another kind of courage, plus a great gaiety of spirit, for her to turn about and say yes to him, in the way and for the reasons she does. She is no Bostonian nymph nor is Darcy a duke, but that is quite a testing adventure they have. And it is most fortunate that Lady Catherine comes barging in with all her celebrated frankness to make it possible for them to bring their adventure to its happy conclusion, a conclusion that is so perfectly appropriate to the qualities of mind and character that they possess as to seem inevitable.

Elizabeth, like Rosalind, Millamant, and Célimène, is lucky (though there is room for arguing about Célimène's luckiness). So, too, are Sara Monday and Moll Flanders and Molly Bloom. So, too, are all of the comic heroes I have discussed. Indeed, what I have called the passivity of these crucial comic characters might well be defined as the capacity to trust in luck. It takes large amounts of luck to survive in this world, and it stands to reason that those who have the patience to wait for luck will experience more of it than those impatient people who try to bend the world to their will. The world, no matter how you define that usefully vague term, is too tough to be bent by any man's will, not even by one as extraordinarily powerful as Ahab's. Melodramatists who see the world as an arena in which to fight to serve their purposes or (same thing) to enforce their will must sooner or later lose, and the odds are it will be sooner rather than later. Furthermore, while they last, life is just one fight after another. Those who have the comic vision perceive, like Joyce Cary in *Art and Reality*, "a reality consisting of permanent and highly obstinate facts, and permanent and highly obstinate human nature," and so they put their trust, obstinately, in their nature rather than in their will. Of course, they, too, will eventually "lose," but only in the sense that they will die. Meanwhile, for however long their "whiles" may be, life for them is a dance, a game, a play, anything but a series of dismal, damned fights.

Thus, the heroes and heroines of comedy are obstinate rather than willful, playful rather than aggressive. They will plot and scheme, but usually with respect only to minor issues and frequently in a deliberately ridiculous way. Rebellions and revolutions, grand defiances and glorious stands, they are likely to leave to others.

One difference between heroes and heroines can be identified. When comedy seeks to assert the primacy of the individual or God over society, or the validity of personal or holy concerns and views over society's concerns and views, it has—perhaps must have—a hero who looks like a fool and often like a coward, too, but who possesses unworldly wisdom and has the courage to go his own way. When comedy seeks to reconcile individual and society, intellect and emotion, or any of the great, linked opposites, it is very likely to have a heroine who is both witty and tender, and who also has the courage, if need be, to go her own way, though she will certainly gather some company along the way.

5.
THE
COMIC SENSE
OF SELF

L ooking one way—from the self out toward the world—the comic vision calls for a stubborn passivity, a willingness to float like a raft going where "it" wants you to go combined with an equally raft-like resistance to any purposeful pushing. Such passivity has nothing to do with apathy or hopelessness or with the neurotic retreats of narcissists from realities they find oppressive; it is adventurous and gay, even when it is colored by desperation.

Looking the other way—from the surface of the self inward—the comic vision calls for another kind of passivity, a negligent disregard for who and what the self may be, a casual assumption that the question of identity is not worth worrying about. A pressing concern for identity is melodramatic, not comic. Seeing reality as an arena for struggle and conflict, the melodramatist must take the question of identity with fierce seriousness, for what is the point of struggling if your identity does not matter? "I am the captain of my fate, I am the master of my soul," proclaims the melodramatist, who wishes to be treated with the respect due a captain. "I am large, I contain multitudes," says the comedian, who does not care which one of the multitude others are regarding at the moment. Paradoxically, comically enough, the more the melodramatist struggles to impose his identity on the world the more he loses his individuality, while the less the comedian worries about who or what he is the more distinctly individual he becomes. It would be hard now to distinguish William Ernest Henley from other Victorian advocates of the stern will, but Walt Whitman remains, even in the midst of all of the writers who have imitated him, unmistakably Walt Whitman.

"Self-negligence" is not a satisfactory term for this fundamental imperative of the comic vision but it is the best, least awkward one available. It points toward the refusal to worry about or fuss over the self that is central in the imperative, and it avoids the misleading implications of a term like "self-acceptance." The self is not something to accept or reject—or to trade in for a new, improved model—it is a "given," though never stable, never permanently fixed. "Negligence" should not be construed as meaning sloppy carelessness. It is not the negligence of a lazy student or that of a dangerous driver; it is more like the negligence of a good athlete who does not have to study the moves he has to make, who just makes them, apparently easily, certainly confidently. Perhaps the comic attitude toward the self can best be compared to the attitude a master woodworker takes toward his valuable cutting tools: they are there for him to use, not to treasure; he will use them when and as he needs them, never abusing them, appreciating them but at the same time taking them for granted.

The reasons comedy demands such an attitude toward the self are many and complex, though all derive from comedy's trust in the finite and concrete. I will explore some of those reasons later in this chapter; for now I simply assert that the major function of the attitude is to render self-pity nearly impossible. From the comic point of view—as far as I can see, from any point of view—self-pity is the most destructive of emotions. It is also the most tempting of emotions, and the most readily available. Anybody, anywhere, at any time, can find a plausible excuse for feeling sorry for himself; in fact, most of us most of the time can lay hold of at least one valid reason. Somebody—mother, father, wife, husband, child, or friend—doesn't love me, at least not enough. My colleagues or my bosses don't appreciate me; I don't receive my just deserts, either in pay or in honors. I am spurned, slighted, and neglected. It's not fair. A fellow as nice as I am shouldn't have to put up with hemorrhoids, or do such work, or pay such taxes. Worst of all, at the end of the dazzlingly long line of excuses or reasons for self-pity lies the inescapable one—I am going to have to die. What a pity! Yet what a warm, sweet, soothing feeling that emotion is; no wonder it is addictive. And no wonder comedy cannot abide it. Its victim is too busy studying himself to pay attention to the world, either to savor its pleasures or avoid its dangers; he has betrayed any trust in either his luck or his wits; and he is useless to himself and to others. Survival is unlikely, but boredom is certain; for though the causes of self-pity are varied and numerous, the emotion itself is singular and monotonous. A comedian can always find something more interesting to do than pity himself.

The comic critique of self-pity is fully and pungently expressed in *The Horse's Mouth*. Both as a painter and as a man Gulley Jimson has plenty of reasons for feeling sorry for himself, but he knows that doing so clogs both his imagination and his arteries. He treats himself with regular, often massive doses of burlesque, invariably referring to self-pity as "the boo-hoos" and giving in only to his most blatantly fraudulent grievances and only in the most preposterous ways. Confronted with a real grievance, the discovery that a painting he had been working on for two years has been tarred over and used to patch holes in a roof, Gulley forces himself to give way to his gaiety. "It's not an easy thing to do when you have a real grievance, and if I had been fifty years younger I shouldn't have done it. But for some time now I had been noticing that on the whole, a man is wise to give way to his gaiety, even at the expense of a grievance. A good grievance is highly enjoyable, but like a lot of other pleasures it is bad for the liver. It affects the digestion and injures the sweetbread. So I gave way and laughed."

For clear and effective illustration of the nature of comic self-negligence I begin where so many of the fundamental images of the comic vision are clearly rendered, with *Don Quixote* and *Huckleberry Finn*. Both books signal the comparative unimportance of identity by giving us a variety of names for their heroes. In the second paragraph of *Don Quixote* (in the Putnam translation) we are told that though some say that the hero's name was Quijada or Quesada, the best conjecture is it was Quejana. A few paragraphs later we are informed that his "real name" must have been Quijada; yet at the very end of the book, when he is dying, the hero firmly proclaims that his name is Alonso Quijana. It does not matter. We know him best by the name he made up for himself, Don Quixote de la Mancha. We also recognize him under the title conferred upon him by his squire, the Knight of the Mournful Countenance, and—

much less certainly—under the title he conferred upon himself, the Knight of the Lions. Huck Finn, too, has plenty of names and identities. He is at various times a girl, Sarah Williams; a runaway bound-servant, George Peters; a boy called George Jackson who is not sure how to spell his name; a nameless English servant boy; and even Tom Sawyer. The son of a remarkably worthless man to whom he bears no resemblance, he learns to model himself on a runaway slave, Jim, who has, of course, no surname.

More interesting, though the two books seem to be in their different ways centrally concerned with the question of their heroes' identities, neither ever really settles the question. The Huck who decides, "All right, then, I'll *go* to hell," is very different from the person who submits to Tom Sawyer's scheme for rescuing Jim. I think we must take his famous final decision to light out for the Territory because Aunt Sally is going to adopt him and "sivilize" him to be, among other things, a firm rejection of the possibility of ever settling into a nice, fixed, "sivilized" identity. Part 1 of *Don Quixote* appears to be asking us to decide whether Quixote is simply a madman with particularly amusing delusions or a man playing at madness with extraordinary intensity and for very deep reasons; yet the best answer it permits us to reach is, "Both or neither," which is no answer at all. Part 2 explores the question of Quixote's identity largely in terms of his relationship with Sancho. It permits, even encourages, us to ask if the gaunt, aristocratic knight who is full of fantastical learning is simply the opposite of his fat, low-born squire who is fantastically full of proverbs; but again the only answer permitted is no answer—yes, no, and maybe. By the end all one can be sure of is that though the two men are startlingly different they are so essentially similar in some ways that they can, when need be, merge or even exchange roles in their relationship. No reader in his right mind would have it otherwise.

The paradoxical result of all of this uncertainty about identity is that the characters project images of great clarity. Even people who have never read the books readily understand the adjective *quixotic* and grasp the significance of describing someone as "Sanchoesque" or "like Huck." Show them a picture of a white boy and a black man on a raft and they will recognize it immediately. Hundreds—possibly thousands—of painters have portrayed Quixote and Sancho and no museum-goer has ever needed to consult a catalog to identify them.

Cervantes was as careless about his own identity as his characters are about theirs. Throughout the novel he claims that he is merely putting into good Spanish a literal translation from an anonymous translator of Benengeli's manuscript, which itself is simply a record of the history of that ingenious gentleman, Don Quixote de la Mancha. More significant, when he wishes to deride the author of the false part 2 he does so by telling the story of the madman who goes about inflating dogs, his inglorious point being that it is no easy thing either to blow up a dog or to write a book like *Don Quixote*. Even on his deathbed Cervantes refused to take himself and his accomplishments seriously. In "Foot in the Stirrup," the short piece he wrote four days before he died, the spokesman for his admirers is a foolish-looking, effusive, fabulously tactless student, and Cervantes gently informs him that he is not "the Muses' darling" or any other glorious thing, but only a man like other men who is facing the common fate, death.

Huck Finn's creator was never so sweetly placid but he most certainly was shifty about his identity. As a man he was Samuel Clemens, Olivia Langdon's loving husband, who was full of lawsuits and of schemes for making a fortune, and who took huge pleasure in being on casual terms with the great of this world; but as an entertainer and artist he was Mark Twain, a sometime pilot, miner, and reporter, who was half boob and half genius, and who was at his best consorting with the lowest of the low.

The comic heroes and heroines I discussed in the last chapter provide more examples of the comic, blurred sense of the self, Ishmael most spectacularly. Elizabeth Bennet may be an exception to the rule, but I think that Elizabeth, like another of Austen's heroines, Emma Woodhouse, is a woman who learns to relax her concern to maintain a clear identity. For further, obvious but diverse examples,

I cite Joyce's Leopold Bloom, Berger's Jack Crabb, and Nabokov's Charles Kinbote (a.k.a. King Charles the Beloved and V. Botkin). For two less obvious but very interesting examples I cite Stendhal's Julien Sorel and Ignazio Silone's Pietro Spina. In *The Red and the Black,* Julien is ridiculous until he abandons his effort to be a Napoleonic man imposing himself on a post-Napoleonic world by donning the uniform of the Church and accepts the truth that he is simply a man who loves Madame de Rênal and who will die. That is, he is ridiculous until he abandons his willful, deeply aggressive enterprise in selfhood and becomes so passive, so unconcerned with identity that even the boundary between life and death becomes unimportant to him. In *Bread and Wine,* Spina returns to Italy sick from tuberculosis and confused by or about all of the certainties on which he has built his identity as a revolutionist; to hide from the Fascist police he becomes a priest, Don Paolo Spada. As Spada, Spina recovers much of his physical strength and loses all of his confusing certainties. At the end of the book, all he knows is that a man must enter into simple, truthful communion with others, who will in turn bestow on him all of the identity he needs.

Looking at all of these characters and at their authors, I conclude that the comic vision requires one to settle for, or cultivate, a blurred, indeterminate sense of one's own identity. Lines of demarcation between the self and the not-self are neither important nor interesting, and they are confining. Drawing them, one becomes cautious and self-protective; ignoring them, one is free to become adventurous and curious. The more carefully one defines one's identity, the more likely the definition is to turn into a cliché. The more protective one is toward the self, the more likely one is to pity oneself. Negligence about identity is likely to be much more liberating; the self is free to become whatever it will become, and there is no point in feeling sorry for a self like that. The true comedian is equally free from self-adoration and self-loathing; consequently, he is also free to endure what must be endured in this world and to savor what may be savored in it.

The comic attitude toward the self can be explained in either

Koestlerian or Lynchian terms. A person who is, for whatever reason, determined to make jokes cannot afford to be engrossed with the self; the sense of identity is the work of consciousness and the would-be joker must penetrate to those areas of mind beneath consciousness where jokes are made. For him, identity is at best a transportation device for getting to those places where jokes are most likely to originate. The serious joker, like the serious scientist and the serious artist, derives whatever importance he has from his work, not from his personality. In Lynchian terms, the comedian is one who has discovered that when he plunges beneath the categories within which most of life is spent he finds that being itself is "profoundly and funnily unbreakable [and] has no needs above itself." Since identity, at least as it is commonly understood, is largely a matter of relating oneself to categories, the true comedian has no need to worry about his identity, and since at rock bottom simple being is good, he has no great need to coddle himself. Identity, to borrow a line from one of Emily Dickinson's comic poems, is just another "overcoat of clay."

But these are explanations of the comic sense of identity in the language of criticism, and we ought to prefer explanations in what Lynch calls the "denser, more cognitive" language of art. That means that we must ultimately go to Walt Whitman and his "Song of Myself," but I turn first to William Carlos Williams, especially to his poem "To Ford Madox Ford in Heaven." Williams is an authoritative source, for he arrived at a finely comic, remarkably careless sense of himself, and he saw Ford Madox Ford as an artist straight out of Rabelais (unlike Hemingway, who portrayed him in *A Moveable Feast* simply as a vain, pompous liar).

Williams's fine memorial tribute to Ford hinges on Williams's belated recognition that he was "a heavenly man," though certainly never a saintly one. That heavenliness was revealed in Ford's writing by his praise of Provence, which, in Williams's phrase, "transubstantiated it from its narrowness to resemble the paths and gardens of a greater world." Williams found it revealed in Ford's life by "a certain grossness" that lived about him.

> The world is cleanly, polished and well
>   made but heavenly man
> is filthy with his flesh and corrupt that
>   loves to eat and drink and whore—
> to laugh at himself and not be afraid of
>   himself knowing well he has
> no possessions and opinions that are worth
>   caring a broker's word about
> and that all he is, but one thing, he feeds
>   as one will feed a pet dog.

The heavenly man finds himself and his world ridiculous; so he clowns with both—grossly—eating, drinking, whoring, laughing, and lying. The saintly man, apparently, takes himself and his world more seriously. Instead of saving only one small part of himself from ruin and of transubstantiating only one small part of the world by means of artistic description, he would purify both himself and his world, struggling to change everything permanently. By comic paradox, Williams implies, the more the saintly man struggles for purity the more worldly he becomes—for the world is "cleanly, polished and well made"—while the careless heavenly man, who knows that he "is homeless here on earth," slips the world's traps and becomes, like Provence, something rare and holy, something individual.

An extra twist to the poem certifies it as true comedy: it forces Williams, who was as little given to conventional religious speculation as a man can be, to work with a term like *transubstantiation*, which reeks of theological hairsplitting, and to take Heaven seriously even though he does not "give a damn for it." Williams may not be as gross as "the fat assed Ford" to whom he pays loving tribute, but he demonstrates that his opinions are not "worth caring a broker's word about" either. The poet is as careless about himself as the Rabelaisian prose writer.

Williams's poems are full of comic, derisive images of himself. "Danse Russe," an early poem, displays him dancing "naked, grotesquely" before his mirror in the morning proclaiming himself "the happy genius of [his] household"; and "To Daphne and Virginia," a late poem, finishes by comparing him to an old pet goose "who waddles, slopping noisily in the mud of his pool." But of course no poet who had any high regard for himself could ever have argued the great importance of a red wheelbarrow.

There is ample evidence that Williams's lack of concern for his own dignity was no pose struck for artistic purposes; unlike Robert Frost, whose private mask was infuriatingly different from the persona of his poems, Williams was essentially the same man outside the poems and stories as in them. In a sense, he *had* to be, for almost from the very beginning (after a brief period of Keatsian effusions) he strove to tie everything he wrote as firmly as possible to the language, gestures, and concerns of his time and place. The stories are in literal fact as well as in fictional device reports snatched from the busy life of a physician; the novels are flat, naturalistic, deliberately unphilosophical accounts of his wife's life; and almost all of the poems, not just *Paterson,* are observations of life as it was lived along the Passaic River in New Jersey during the first half of the twentieth century. The physician might have been gruff and unsentimental with his patients, but he never treated them in a condescending manner. The poet might have been shrilly furious about T. S. Eliot's enormous success because he thought it was taking American poetry in the wrong direction, but he was consistently, even extravagantly generous in his response to younger writers who needed help getting started. Williams's biographer, Reed Whittemore, reports—with some annoyance and perhaps a dash of incomprehension—that in his old age, when he was finally getting some decent measure of praise and recognition, Williams kept insisting on his own commonplaceness. After his death in 1963, Hugh Kenner, in a memorial essay published in the *National Review* (14:237), spoke eloquently of his "innocence and aching vulnerability," his ability to go "unprotected by any public role."

There is no sure, easy way of explaining how such a man could develop such a relationship with himself, but I think that one of Williams's deepest explorations into the heart of the matter is his poem "The Descent." It is a meditation on the image of descent, the product of years of disciplined dedication to the creed ''no ideas but in things''; but it can also be described as a fine example of the analogical imagination dealing in its fundamentally concrete way with a matter that the univocal mind can deal with only weakly and abstractly. In this poem Williams sees that ''the descent beckons as the ascent beckoned'' and that ''memory is a kind of accomplishment, a sort of renewal even an initiation.'' Consequently, ''no defeat is made up entirely of defeat,'' for it always opens up new memories (or new ways of remembering) and new, hitherto unsuspected possibilities. Thus, the various defeats the body suffers as one descends into old age open up the possibility of ways of loving that are much less shadowed and distorted by desire. The conclusion is triumphant:

> The descent
> > made up of despairs
> > > and without accomplishment
> > realizes a new awakening:
> > > > which is a reversal
> > of despair.
> > > > For what we cannot accomplish, what
> > is denied to love,
> > > > what we have lost in the anticipation—
> > > > > a descent follows,
> > > endless and indestructible

A man who lives in a reality like that, where ascent and descent, victory and defeat are equally to be relished, has not the slightest need to worry about himself; the more he takes himself as someone common and unimportant, the more surely he is on the track of something endless and indestructible.

No wonder Williams can say that he does not care a damn for Heaven. In his own very distinct, un-transcendental way he can exclaim with Thoreau, ''Talk of heaven! ye disgrace earth.''

But behind Williams looms Whitman, and it is Whitman who gives the densest, most cognitive, most comprehensive account of the comic vision of the self. Indeed, there is more of it in *Leaves of*

Grass than I can do justice to here. For an adequately detailed discussion one can go to E. Fred Carlisle's book *The Uncertain Self: Whitman's Drama of Identity* (1973). Carlisle's vocabulary is different from mine because he works with a typology taken from Martin Buber's exploration of the *I-Thou* relation; but since he finally stresses the "open" or "uncertain" quality of Whitman's ideal self, I think our conclusions are essentially the same.

I begin with "Crossing Brooklyn Ferry," where Whitman makes high comedy out of his realization that he cannot be sure where the self ends and the not-self begins. He acknowledges that the Walt Whitman lounging at the rail of the ferry is quite separate from the others who have crossed, are crossing, or will cross to Brooklyn on the ferry. Yet he sees the obvious truth that he and the others are sharing the same experience, and he knows that each of us in part, though not in whole, is the product of his experience. If he himself is altered by his perception of the things of the river and harbor—the oscillating wings of the sea gulls, the scallop-edged waves, the shimmering track of beams of sunlight, the swinging motion of the hulls of boats and ships—then others must also be altered by their perceptions of the same inescapable presences, and altered in similar ways. Consequently, he must share identity, however minutely, with all of those who have had the experience, and especially with those who have had the experience vicariously while reading his poem. By the end of the eighth section, the distance between Whitman and the reader, between "I" and the "you" he can address with startling directness, is zero. (Or, to use the phrase Carlisle takes from Buber, it is clear that the two are standing together on that "narrow ridge where *I* and *Thou* meet.") He is justified, then, in concluding the poem with an extraordinary lyric on the *things* seen from the ferry, celebrating them as "dumb, beautiful ministers" that we plant permanently within us and that furnish their parts "toward eternity" and "toward the soul."

Perhaps I should emphasize, as Carlisle does, that Whitman's identity is only uncertain or indeterminate, not indiscriminate. If on one side it merges with the things of this world and with the other living beings in it, on the other side it remains a visibly solitary singer from Long Island. Whitman was not at all like those guru-smitten, would-be mystics of our time that Gita Mehta satirizes in *Karma Cola: Marketing the Mystic East* (1979) who seek a dose of esoterica that will relieve them of the burden of identity. He seeks "amplitude" for his identity, extending it until he knows that it is "tenon'd and mortis'd in granite" and he is free to "laugh at . . . dissolution."

The amplitude is dealt with most fully in "Song of Myself." There, in those long catalogs that exasperate impatient readers, he drives home the truth that one shares identity with all sorts of persons in all sorts of circumstances. And there he celebrates exuberantly the fusion of self with the things and creatures of the earth: "I find I incorporate gneiss, coal, long-threaded moss, fruits, grains, esculent roots, and am stucco'd with quadrupeds and birds all over." And there, too, he states, assumes, dramatizes, and argues the self's share of divinity. The pronoun "I" in "Song of Myself" has a dazzling collection of antecedents. In only a relatively few places does it refer simply to Whitman—and then he is described not so simply as a "kosmos, of Manhattan the son." Mostly that "I" ranges over the world and even the universe, referring to various men and to women, to the high and the low, the living and the dead, to pismires, tree-toads, and mice, to rocks and grains of sand, to all of the gods, and to God. By the time one comes to the famous aside near the end of the poem, "I am large, I contain multitudes," it seems almost a modest understatement.

The great implication that arises from this amplitude is that the self can be perfectly at ease with the certainty of death. "To die is different from what anyone supposed, and luckier." That is the claim that most baffles and annoys many of Whitman's readers, the naive and the sophisticated alike. Different, maybe, but luckier? The naive express their skepticism and annoyance directly, in muttered, frequently scatological asides; the sophisticated are more circumspect but finally, I think, no less outraged. They know that there is a large body of religious literature on the unimportance of death, and they do not mind so much when Whitman expresses his conviction in "Out of the Cradle Endlessly Rocking" and "When Lilacs Last in the Dooryard Bloom'd," because he seems appropriately solemn and metaphysical in those poems. But in "Song of Myself" he insists on taking mortality—ours as well as his—comically, as though it really were a joking matter, and with cocky disregard for all canons of taste.

> And as to you Death, and you bitter hug of mortality, it is idle to try
>   to alarm me.
> To his work without flinching the accoucheur comes,
> I see the elder-hand pressing receiving supporting,
> I recline by the sills of the exquisite flexible doors,
> And mark the outlet, and mark the relief and escape.
> And as to you corpse I think you are good manure, but that does not
>   offend me,
> I smell the white roses sweet-scented and growing.
> I reach to the leafy lips, I reach to the polish'd
> breasts of melons.

What a mixed bag those lines are for a person of good taste! First there is the clumsy, unnecessary borrowing from French, *accoucheur,* and then he links it with an old-fashioned, Quakerish term, *elderhand.* "The sills of the exquisite flexible doors" may strike one as a fine descriptive metaphor for the vulva of a woman giving birth, assuming that one grants the need for such description, but does he have to insist with grotesque vividness on "reclining" by those doors? Similarly, "the polish'd breasts of melons" is at once a fresh and an inevitable figure of speech, but the lines insist on connecting it with the image of a corpse that is good "manure." Thus, a discriminating reader can justify dismissing these lines, yet the suspicion persists that what people recoil from here—and in the many similar passages in "Songs of Myself"—is not so much Whitman's vulgarity of diction and reference as his buoyant conviction that mortality really is unthreatening, even beneficent. He is so convinced of that truth he does not even argue it, he simply displays it, dances with it. He casually mixes images of birth and death, sexuality and defecation, and corruption and nutrition because he does not *feel* the need to be precise and delicate in dealing with such a glorious and self-evident truth. And he is right not to. To let precision and delicacy intrude here would be a betrayal of the truth he has seen. From the very beginning of "Song of Myself" Whitman recognizes that he must hold "creeds and schools in abeyance"; for good or bad his obligation is to let speak "at every hazard, nature without check with original energy." Speaking symbolically in section 2, he says that he must get away from "perfumes," though he knows them and likes them. Speaking in a parable in section 11, he laments the fate of the twenty-ninth bather, the woman who must hide "aft the blinds of the window" when she yearns to be down on the beach with the twenty-eight young men. And speaking as directly as possible in section 32, he says that he "could turn and live with animals" because "not one is respectable or unhappy over the whole earth." "Song of Myself," indeed the whole *Leaves of Grass*, is deliberately and necessarily vulgar, antipathetic in every way to genteel considerations, rightly described as a "barbaric yawp" sounded "over the roofs of the world."

Whitman's vulgarity is deeply connected with his attitude toward death. It is certainly necessary to the accurate expression of the attitude; it may actually be the product of the attitude. In any event, it is misleading to discuss his vulgarity simply in terms of his rebellion against nineteenth-century prudery; he was digging deeper than that, into the very roots of what came to be known later as genteel culture. Prudery was only its flower—or better, its emblem, the outward and visible manifestation of its inner and spiritual state. The outward avoidance of sexuality stood for the inner avoidance of everything that leveled the precious or distinguished, rendering it common and, apparently, valueless. In the nineteenth century, the genteel feared that candid acceptance of sexuality would destroy the whole structure of attitudes that preserved their self-importance; in the twentieth century, we know better. Now, one can be shockingly liberated about sexuality and still safely genteel, secure in the knowledge that the best people can copulate like monkeys without endangering their bestness. But Whitman with his damnably cocky, even arrogant embrace of everything that levels bestness, including the great leveler death, remains a threat to the genteel. They are well advised to be outraged by him.

If I seem to have wandered from my theme in these last few paragraphs, I have not. "Song of Myself," "Crossing Brooklyn Ferry," and many other poems in *Leaves of Grass* give a coherent and penetrating account of the comic sense of identity. That sense of identity is characterized by a cheerful lack of concern about drawing boundary lines between the self and the not-self, and a full acceptance of one's own mortality seems to be crucial. Comic identities are always a threat to genteel or official (the two terms are nearly synonymous) traditions of culture. Acceptance of mortality, of the mutability of the self as well as of the world, is a fundamental theme of comedy. For a lyrical expression of the theme one cannot do better than the ending of "Song of Myself":

> The last scud of day holds back for me,
> It flings my likeness after the rest and true as any on the shadow'd
>   wilds,
> It coaxes me to the vapor and the dusk.
> I depart as air, I shake my white locks at the runaway sun,
> I effuse my flesh in eddies, and drift it in lacy jags.
> I bequeath myself to the dirt to grow from the grass I love,
> If you want me again look for me under your boot-soles.
> You will hardly know who I am or what I mean,
> But I shall be good health to you nevertheless,
> And filter and fibre your blood.
> Failing to fetch me at first keep encouraged,
> Missing me one place search another,
> I stop somewhere waiting for you.

We can now return with clearer understanding to the paradox of individuality growing from a comic carelessness about the identity of the self. It comes from the comedian's compulsion to reach out to the finite, as Whitman does in "Crossing Brooklyn Ferry," as Williams does in "The Descent," to find out what is in it for him and of him.

He does this time after time, in large matters and small, until whatever identity he has is in significant part an amalgam of all the people, places, and things he has reached out for. When he regards himself, he sees—rightly—something commonplace; when we regard him, we see—equally rightly—something distinctly individual. The logic of the situation is obvious. The finite is the domain of the unique: every oak tree is finally different from every other oak tree, no matter how much they might resemble each other. Thus, the finite is more subtle and more complex than any generalization that can be made about it. Therefore, an identity grounded in the finite must be more nearly unique, more individual than an identity grounded in any set of generalizations, no matter what their sources, no matter whether they appear to be moral injunctions, religious revelations, or scientific truths. To urge people to develop ''strong self-images'' or to do either their ''duty'' or ''their own thing'' is to lead them into prefabricated boxes where they may smother. To tell them to ''lean and loafe . . . observing a spear of summer grass'' or to exclaim to them, ''no ideas but in things!'' is to lead them toward an open world in which they can flourish.

Whitman and Williams flourished, each in his own distinct way. It is impossible to imagine Whitman ever having the intellectual and personal discipline to submit to medical training and to maintain a medical practice; it is equally impossible to imagine Williams enduring the downright sloppiness of Whitman's life as a journalist in the years before he was ready to begin *Leaves of Grass* or managing so cheerfully to pass away years of invalidism ''gassing'' with Horace Traubel in Camden. There was an abundance of the old-fashioned ham in Whitman, as one can see by the variety of poses he struck for photographers; Williams was made of leaner, tougher stuff and was too intent on doing whatever he was doing to enjoy striking poses. Also, of course, they differed in their sexual natures. Whitman was more strongly attracted to men than to women; Williams was thoroughly heterosexual, and his relationship with his wife, Flossie, was at the center of both his life and his work. But different as they were, they were both true comedians. Free from fear of time and of mortality, they were free of self-pity. They were therefore free to take themselves as jokes and to pursue all of the images arising out of those jokes. They could not possibly capture all of those images—jokes are long and life is short. But they did get an astonishing amount of work done. The comic vision is not for the lazy or the delicate.

The idea that one ought to take a negligent attitude toward oneself, to treat the question of identity carelessly, is at odds with the ideas about self and identity that are dominant in contemporary culture. It particularly conflicts with the contemporary tendency to see the artist as a self-assertive hero who acts out and validates our own half-repressed desire for unqualified independence. Ultimately that view of the artist derives from the original romantic exaltation of the individual, especially of his will; from Shelley and Byron on we have had many romantic artists who may rightly be seen—who saw themselves—as acting out the possibility of independence from a society that would constrict us all. But in our time, with the set of yearnings and beliefs that Christopher Lasch has described in *The Culture of Narcissism* (1979), the need to see the artist as one who imposes his self upon the world has become intense. Witness the public images of those artists who have become celebrities. Ernest Hemingway was, as Norman Mailer is, an obvious example, but even long-dead artists have been reprocessed into celebrities to fulfill narcissistic needs. Emily Dickinson, complex and baffling as she actually was, has been made into a heroine for the women's liberation movement, and Henry David Thoreau became a father figure for radicals in the late sixties because he spent a night in jail to protest the Mexican War—all concerned conveniently forgetting that he spent the next morning leading a huckleberrying party.

Yet artists as well as their fictional heroes and heroines, not to mention uncelebrated people who live their lives in the light of the comic vision, have responded to a comic imperative to take the self as means, not end, as less important and less interesting than the not-self. Thoreau is a fine example. When he practiced what he and Emerson called ''self reliance'' by moving out to Walden Pond his purpose was "to front only the essential facts of *life*," not to discover and publicize the identity of Henry David Thoreau; and though he most certainly did retain "the *I*, or first person," in his book, he paid far more attention to the ripples of the water in the pond than to the flutters of his psyche. Thoreau had too much comic sense to take himself solemnly, a fact that he proclaimed in the epigraph to *Walden:* "I do not propose to write an ode to dejection, but to brag as lustily as chanticleer in the morning, standing on his roost, if only to wake my neighbors up."

There are many artists whose lives and works become more comprehensible and therefore more valuable to us when we force aside the notion that the artist is necessarily a model of self-assertion and realize that he may well be a model of self-negligence. To test that thesis, but also to gain a more concrete understanding of what self-negligence means and of how it relates to other comic ideas and attitudes, I consider two twentieth-century writers that contemporary American criticism has had difficulty categorizing—Georges Simenon and H. L. Mencken.

Simenon is popular with readers almost everywhere in the world; his novels have been translated from their original French into thirty-five to forty different languages, and other novelists, ranging from André Gide to Henry Miller, have testified to the quality of his work, as have a number of English and European critics. But in this country we have not known what to do with him. Despite the fact that more than thirty of his short, subtle psychological novels have been published here in the last decade (by Harcourt Brace Jovanovich), we have classified him as a mystery writer, because a large number of his Inspector Maigret novels have also appeared in that decade, and we have mostly ignored him. We have not so much ignored Mencken as consigned him to literary history, as though he were important only for the work he did in the 1920s as an editor and literary critic. Yet his writing remains alive and widely read. That includes the journalism he produced throughout his career, the polemics that he wrote mainly in the 1920s, the massive studies of the

American language that he published in the 1930s and 1940s, and the biographical essays that he wrote between 1936 and 1943.

As a novelist, Simenon has been fascinated with characters who possess or are reaching toward the simplest possible identities for themselves, and as a man, he has struggled to keep his own identity simple and undefined despite the pressures generated by his successful career. Though we have ignored him, the European press has not, and he has been the subject of innumerable articles in newspapers and magazines. The result of such popularity is the same there as it is here: the man is threatened with imprisonment within his success, especially with the psychic imprisonment of having to live within the limits of his popular image. In Simenon's case, there is a well-developed legend of him as a writer who uses his now enormous wealth to keep himself remote from the concerns of ordinary life and who organizes every detail of his life with almost neurotic rigidity so that he may produce his several novels a year—at least, that was the image that prevailed until he announced his retirement from fiction writing in 1973 when he was seventy years old.

When I Was Old (1971) is a record of his protest against that image and of his struggle to maintain his own quite different sense of his identity. It is a series of notebooks that he began keeping in 1960, when he rather suddenly began to feel old, and stopped keeping in 1962, when with equal suddenness he stopped feeling old. A string of interviewers, all asking the same trite questions, all determined to cut him to fit the legend, seems to have played a major part in bringing on that feeling. Simenon proves that he has recovered from it when he writes sincerely—and persuasively—"What would humiliate me most would be to have unconsciously wound up taking myself seriously" (p. 339). He has reestablished his deepest conviction that he is a man like other men, possessing no special wisdom, knowing no more than anyone else why he does what he does, let alone what it all "means." True, he writes novels and most men do not, but he sees no great merit in that distinction. He is "of the family of those who devote their time to trying to better man's life, no matter what man'' (p. 22); and since he happens to have "a certain lucidity which makes [him] see causes and effects at the same time" (p. 140), the best contribution he can make is to write novels that can show to every man his identity with other men, thereby releasing him from shame or pride or anguish over his own particular life. If he boasts of anything it is that as a novelist he is a naturalist rather than a philosopher, dealing in patient observation rather than in ideas (p. 32). "Intelligence explains all. Falsely. As if it were arithmetic" (p. 62). So he exclaims in a spirit his friend Henry Miller would understand and applaud, "Shit on abstract ideas!" (p. 244).

So much in many of Simenon's novels is so grim that it may be hard to accept the word "comic" in connection with his image of himself or of reality. But he argues in several places in *When I Was Old* that he is an optimist, not a pessimist, and his views throughout the book parallel those that William Lynch ascribes to comedy, even to the point of his wondering if it may not "be necessary or indispensable that a man touch bottom at least once in his life to become wholly a man" (p. 219). More explicit evidence of the validity of the term comes from two of his fictions, *Maigret's Memoirs* and *The Little Saint*.

Maigret's Memoirs (1963) is a book that Cervantes would approve of, for it blurs the distinction between fact and fiction in something of the same way that part 2 of *Don Quixote* does. Here, Maigret speaks for himself (the other books in the Maigret series are in the third person) and does so in order to correct the oversimplified—and sometimes mistaken—picture that Simenon has given of him. If he finally concludes, under his wife's prompting, that what he says about himself is not all that different from what Simenon has said, he has had the satisfaction of correcting the minor errors that would ruffle a man—for example, Simenon's showing him wearing a bowler hat and an overcoat with a velvet collar long after he had discarded them—and of asserting the importance to him of matters that are scarcely touched on in the books, such as his father's work as the manager of a large estate and his own pride in being part of officialdom. He has also had the satisfaction of gently mocking

THE COMIC SENSE OF SELF

Simenon—for being the excessively cocky young man he was when the series started and for over the years coming to resemble Maigret in the way he walks and smokes his pipe and even in the way he talks.

The resemblance, though, goes much deeper than that, as one can see by comparing this genial little book, written in 1950, with *When I Was Old*. Maigret, too, feels that he is simply a man like other men, and he displays little of the self-absorption that characterizes people who are anxious to define their identities. Even in his memoirs, he gives much more weight and space to the life around him than to his own thoughts and feelings and accomplishments. And his reply to those who ask if he does not feel disgusted by all the sordid people his work brings him into contact with is similar to Simenon's own response to those who think he has been rendered pessimistic by the reality he has observed in his novels: "No, I don't! And it's probably through my job that I have acquired a fairly unshakeable optimism" (p. 152).

The Little Saint (1965) speaks almost as directly to the same points. It is an account of the life of a painter, Louis Cuchas, dealing mostly with his childhood in one of the poorest sections of Paris and with the years when without any awareness of doing anything notable he gradually became a painter rather than a worker in the sheds at Les Halles. Simenon, in remarks quoted on the dust jacket of the American edition, saw it as a triumphant breakthrough, as the novel in which he was finally able "to exteriorize a certain optimism that is in me, a *joie de vivre,* a delight in the immediate and simple communion with all that surrounds me." Louis, who is plainly another, though deeply hidden, side of Simenon, is a remarkably passive, unselfconscious person. He first acquires the nickname "The Little Saint" in school because he does not fight back at the bigger boys who take his marbles and push him around; he reacquires it as an adult because, still very small, he is completely unconcerned about money and fame. However, he is not saintly in any of the conventional ways. He has no religious beliefs or concerns; and though he is himself shy, he does not see any sin in sexuality. In fact, he does not pass any judgment on anyone's behavior; he is too busy trying to paint the reality that he sees to worry about things like that. Thus, he is rendered unworldly by the purity of his absorption in the world that lies immediately around him. To all questions about why he did this or what that means he replies, "I don't know." His thoughts and his purposes are unimportant, but when someone suggests that the objects he paints are unimportant to him, he promptly replies, "My cabbages, my beef, my little train are *very* important" (p. 163). At the end of the novel, when he is old and famous, he is asked, most respectfully, how he sees himself; he has to pause for a moment, because it has never occurred to him to ask that question himself, and is delighted to discover that the answer is "As a small boy."

Simenon is much more complicated and much more worldly than his painter, Louis Cuchas—a novelist must be. Yet in *Letter to My Mother* (1974), a memoir that he dictated, not wrote, after he retired from fiction, he concluded that he, too, should see himself as a child of sorts. The "letter" records his efforts to understand and accept his painful relationship with his mother as she lay dying at ninety-one. She was, he belatedly realizes, an extraordinarily complicated woman who was driven by a ferocious need to be good and who therefore sacrificed herself for every unfortunate who came along. She wasted little of her patience and tenderness on him, once he was past childhood, because she saw him as a "spoiled darling of fortune," as one of those "who have everything." And now he knows that she was right—right not to waste her gifts on him, right that he is fortune's child, who has no real need for the tenderness that in self-pitying moments he had wanted from her.

No one, least of all Georges Simenon, has the right to feel sorry for Georges Simenon. He has lived his life in a world that he has found much more interesting than himself, and he has completed an immense amount of work. No other novelist can match what he calls his "mosaic of small novels," which consists of well over two hundred pieces. Naturally, inevitably, some of those are not as good as others, but the best of them are astonishingly powerful and even the run-of-the-mill novels command respect. Moreover, all of them are distinctly his own, unlike anybody else's work. His name, his identity, is stamped all over every page he has ever published.

It is a long jump in time, space, and temperament from Georges Simenon in his mansion in Switzerland to H. L. Mencken in his family's house on Hollins Street in Baltimore, yet some of the things I have said about Simenon can also be said about Mencken. Certainly, he produced a prodigious amount of work, too—dozens of books, hundreds of magazine pieces, thousands of letters, and hundreds of thousands of column inches of newspaper articles—and just as certainly, it all carried his distinctive mark. In the 1920s when he was supplying large amounts of copy for the *Smart Set* and the *American Mercury,* which he also edited in whole or part, he used a variety of *noms de plume,* but no one ever was fooled by them. Whatever he wrote read like it could have been written only by H. L. Mencken.

Simenon took a popular form of fiction and made it serve his own artistic purposes. Twisting it one way, he made it into a ''Simenon,'' a short, intense psychological novel in which he plunges himself and his reader deep into the causes or the consequences of an act of violence; twisting it another way, he made it into a ''Maigret,'' a sketch of a milieu and a character. The Simenons are oil paintings by an extraordinary portraitist; the Maigrets are his watercolors and pencil sketches. A few youthful experiments aside, Mencken never worked in a recognized art form, but he wrote journalism, literary criticism, social commentary, histories of ideas, philology, and memoirs as though he were writing art. Refusing to recognize that reporting is supposed to be ephemeral and philology dull, he supplied the Baltimore *Sun* with stories about the Scopes trial that nearly sixty years later are still interesting and informative, and he discussed the vagaries of American speech in *The American Language* in paragraphs that are both accurate and funny. Everything he wrote he wrote with enormous comic zest, throwing himself so fully into the piece at hand as to half convince a reader of its permanent importance. The curious result is that when you read his literary criticism you are driven to think of him as primarily a literary critic, and when you read his social criticism you know that his mission in life was to rid American society of puritanical foolishness. He was never really an intellectual, but he could juggle ideas so clearly and so cleverly that it is hard not to think of him as an ideologue. Nor was he ever truly a scholar, but he absorbed so much scholarship so quickly and so completely that *The American Language* became something close to a model of scholarship.

However, in all forms and at all times Mencken was a comedian. This is not to classify him as a humorist, though a remarkably large number of the pages he wrote had jokes in or lurking near them. Nor is it to deny the seriousness of his social criticism or the force of his attack on puritanism in general and the genteel culture in particular. It is simply to recognize the obvious truth that what makes a piece by Mencken plainly Mencken's, no matter what name he may have signed to it, is its playfulness, its refusal to take things simply and solemnly. He played with ideas and attitudes, with sensitivities and sensibilities, with the pieties of his culture and the expectations of his readers, with the vanity of his opponents and the dignity of his supporters, and—above all—with language. His knowledge of American English was both copious and exact, and he was nearly incapable of writing two sentences in a row without playing the tone of one word or phrase off another.

Mencken was best known during his lifetime for the essays of opinion that appeared, in book form, in a series of six volumes under the forthright title *Prejudices*. They were exuberant, noisy assaults on the ''booboisie'' (to use his most famous coinage) and they gave a generation of readers the glorious feeling that they really were free to think and say whatever they wanted to think and say about any subject whatsoever. The best of them—for example, ''The Hills of Zion,'' an account of the fundamentalists who flocked to Dayton, Tennessee, for the Scopes trial—still work vividly, but most have faded with time because they attack people and mock attitudes that are largely forgotten. The essays in *Prejudices* also labor under a less obvious difficulty: they required Mencken, for his polemic purposes, to strike the pose of an aristocrat, a member of the natural elite who are too fastidious to join in the swinishness of the democratic herd.

Few people were ever fooled by that pose, if only because he so plainly lacked the malice and impenetrable smugness of a true elitist. Still, the best of his essays are those in which he abandoned polemics and the pose that they required and gave free vent to his comic sense of self and of the life he had lived. These essays were gathered in three volumes, *Happy Days* (1940), *Newspaper Days* (1941), and *Heathen Days* (1943). (*A Choice of Days*, 1980, is a one-volume selection that I had the pleasure of editing, but everyone who has sense enough and time will not settle for a one-third measure.)

Before discussing what is in these books, let me stress what is not in them. There is nothing to suggest that there was anything unusual about Mencken's career and accomplishments. A reader of *Newspaper Days* can gather that he rose from cub reporter to editor of a metropolitan daily in only a few years, but that success is treated as a happy accident, which is much less important than the fact that he led "the gaudy life" of a young reporter in an American city at the turn of the century, "the maddest, gladdest, damndest existence ever enjoyed by mortal youth" (p. 18). And the only reference in *Heathen Days* to his career as an editor, first of the *Smart Set* and then of the *American Mercury*, is an acknowledgement that "during the whole of the twelve years, ten months and nineteen days" of Prohibition he was a magazine editor and hence subject to melancholia. Otherwise, he is simply a man who had the great good luck to be born into a loving family in Baltimore in 1880 and who subsequently got to know many interesting, amusing people from all walks of life. *Happy Days* is obviously the right title for the first volume, which deals with his childhood, but as he belatedly realized, that would have been the right title for the other two books, too. In other words, there is nothing in any of the books to indicate that he was ever anything but a lucky, happy man with no cause ever to feel sorry for himself. Yet when Mencken began writing these happy essays he was a fifty-five-year-old man whose great reputation and influence had suddenly evaporated and whose wife had died, only five years after they had married, of spinal meningitis. Very few men in such circumstances could resist pitying themselves, but Mencken did not believe in self-pity. That is a very good thing, for in November 1948 he suffered a massive stroke, which, with massive irony, centered on the part of his brain that controlled language. He lived seven more years, but he was never able to read or to write, or even to speak other than haltingly. Though surely there was not a day during those seven hideously frustrating years when he would not have died gladly, he endured them without whining.

Through most of his autobiographical essays Mencken is too busy memorializing the hostlers, hack drivers, back-alley philosophers, cops, magistrates, reporters, publicity men, politicians, bartenders, and preachers who deliberately or inadvertently made his days amusing to pay much attention to himself. When he does give an image of himself it is almost always derisive. Talking about his ''Introduction to the Universe'' in *Happy Days,* he reports that ''there is a picture of me at eighteen months which looks like a picture the milk companies print in the rotogravure section of the Sunday papers, whooping up the zeal of their cows. If cannibalism hadn't been abolished in Maryland some years before my birth I'd have butchered beautifully'' (p. 7). He is no more impressed with his forty-four-year-old self, for in ''The Noble Experiment'' (*Heathen Days*) he tells of trying to talk his way past a suspicious doorman in a speakeasy in Bethlehem, Pennsylvania, by pointing out that no Prohibition agent ever looked ''so innocent, so moony, so dumb'' as he does (p. 206).

The derision extends even to the class with which Mencken identifies himself. ''I was,'' he states in the preface to *Happy Days,* ''a larva of the comfortable and complacent bourgeoisie, though I was quite unaware of the fact until I was along in my teens, and had begun to read indignant books. To belong to that great order of mankind is vaguely discreditable today, but I still maintain my dues-paying membership in it, and continue to believe that it was and is authentically human, and therefore worthy of the attention of philosophers, at least to the extent that the Mayans, Hittites, Kallikuks and so on are worthy of it'' (p. viii). That's Mencken. Loyal to his family, enjoying his comfort, and always refusing to be a reformer, he gladly affirms his membership in the bourgeoisie, but he insists on finding it as comic as he finds himself and the rest of the world.

Mencken lacked self-importance, not self-respect. His test of any man or woman, himself included, was competence. ''I simply can't imagine competence as anything save admirable, for it is very rare in this world, and especially in this great Republic, and those who have it in some measure, in any art or craft from adultery to zoology, are the only human beings I can think of who will be worth the oil it will take to fry them in Hell'' (*Heathen Days*, p. viii). All three of the *Days* reflect his admiration for competence and they reach comic heights in celebrating its manifestation in unlikely persons and forms: in champion beer drinkers, in an all-night hack driver who takes a naive girl from Red Lion, P.A., who thinks she has been doomed to a life of sin to a Madame who will not exploit her, and even in a mayor of San Francisco (James Rolph, Jr.) who made the Democratic National Convention of 1920 a pure delight by soothing the delegates and reporters with carloads of absolutely first class Bourbon whiskey. Certainly he respected his own competence as a newspaperman, as a magazine editor, and as a prose writer. He was very good at his jobs, and he knew that he could hold his head up in the company of the best adulterers or zoologists.

Competence was what Mencken respected. What he loved was the American language. He contemplated, studied, analyzed, categorized, exercised, chastised, embraced, adored, celebrated, and enlarged it as faithfully and as playfully as any fond lover in history. His monument to that love was *The American Language,* especially the so-called ''fourth edition,'' and the two supplements to it. But his record of and tribute to that love is both finer and more copious— all of the hundreds of thousands of sentences he wrote in the fifty years between the day in 1898 that the Baltimore *Herald* published his first piece of reporting and the day in 1948 that he was muted by a stroke. Even those first two sentences were good enough to be beyond improvement by a rewrite man: ''A horse, a buggy, and several sets of harness, valued in all at about $250, were stolen last night from the stable of Howard Quinlan, near Kingsville. The county police are at work on the case, but so far no trace of either thieves or booty has been found.'' Of the prodigious number of sentences that followed, inevitably some were silly and some were trite, but all, I think, were written to come smoothly off an American tongue and fall comfortably on an American ear. By the time he came to write the *Days* essays he seems to have become actually incapable of formulating a twisted, awkward sentence. What a state of grace for a writer to attain!

Self-negligence is, either explicitly or implicitly, a primary theme in the works of Simenon and Mencken, and in their lives, too. Neither could have written so much had he been concerned with discovering and asserting his own identity. Self-assertion is an exhausting and finally unrewarding business. Artists who are too engrossed in the life around them to worry about who and what they are, are free to make a quixotic attempt to explore entire worlds; they fail, of course, but they get an enormous amount of work done, and without at all intending to do so, they fully establish their own individuality. They may be like P. G. Wodehouse, who lived what I would have to describe as a resolutely dull life, but who published more than ninety books, a remarkable number of which remain very funny. He was more than halfway through another novel when he died in 1975, some four months past his ninety-third birthday. Or they may be like Joyce Cary, who when he found that he was suffering from an incurable disease, a progressive muscular atrophy, abandoned his plans for a trilogy and tried to pack it all into a single book. He could not quite finish *The Captive and the Free* (1958) before his illness made it literally impossible for him to write. As a novel it has its faults, but it is free of any glimmer of self-pity or any other self-concern, as was everything he ever wrote. Renoir and Matisse also furnish good examples of comic self-negligence. When Renoir was so crippled by arthritis that he had to tie the brushes to his hand and take twenty minutes to raise his arm to the canvas he did his *Bathers* and a number of other equally serene paintings. When Matisse became bedridden he worked on his cutouts of colored paper, and with charcoal fixed to the end of a bamboo rod he sketched on pieces of paper pinned to the ceiling of his bedroom. Duke Ellington would do for an example, too. He did his last composing in a hospital room while he was dying of cancer; most of the rest of his voluminous body of work he had written in hotels, trains, and automobiles during the decades he was on the road with his band.

Self-negligence is not something on the order of a sweet and saintly forbearance of selfish pleasure; there was little or none of that in most of the writers I have cited as examples. Mencken relished the pleasures that were important to him, especially music, beer, and Baltimore crab dishes; and Simenon's third wife, Denise, has portrayed him as a most unsaintly sexual athlete and a bear to live with. Let that flamboyantly unsugary, unsaintly comedian W. C. Fields serve as a final exemplar of the comic attitude toward the self. As William Claude Dukinfield he suffered through a childhood and adolescence that seemed guaranteed to leave its victim wallowing in self-pity. So he invented a new identity for himself as W. C. Fields and made it so preposterous, so shabby, so full of petty treachery that no one could be tempted to pity him, not even himself. In *It's a Gift, The Bank Dick,* and the other film comedies that he made he used that blatantly fraudulent identity as a means of deriding all of the fraudulent pieties of American popular culture.

One thing is certain: the comic attitude toward the self is the opposite of a narcissistic one. Comedy forbids self-adoration, as it forbids self-loathing, and as it forbids self-pity; narcissism puts the three together in one dismal triangle. Comedy agrees with Thoreau that "any truth is better than make-believe"; narcissism on any of its sides is a form of make-believe. Anybody who thinks he is worthy of adoration is ignoring much of what he is and much of what he does; anybody who has not found more suitable objects for either pity or loathing simply has not looked. The comic vision requires that those who live by it welcome, however ruefully, time and change; narcissism calls for a struggle against time, which is futile, and a fear of change, which is pathetic. Narcissism, like other forms of make-believe, is finally boring. The self, especially the carefully cultivated self, is too limited, too lacking in variety to remain interesting over any long haul; the imagination and the mind need more to work with than the self alone can provide. Even the senses are betrayed into dullness by narcissism's focus on the response rather than on the stimulus: the more carefully you observe responses, the more you tend to discover uniformity; the more carefully you observe stimuli, the more you tend to discover infinite variety. That is what Cleopatra knew—and Shakespeare, too, of course.

The comic vision with its demand for self-negligence can be hard on those who attempt to live by it. There are no guarantees in life, and the comedian knows as well as the tragedian that you can count no man lucky until he is dead. Yet the jaunty examples of the comic heroes and heroines discussed in the last chapter and of the comic artists discussed in this one suggest that comic self-negligence can have high medicinal value. It will not cure all the ills that mind and flesh are heir to, but it will preserve you from boredom and give you a chance to be useful to yourself and to others.

6.
COMEDY
AND
INJUSTICE

omedy's strategy for dealing with self-pity is straightforward and manageable: one simply and rigorously shuns the emotion. Given even the best, the most powerfully tempting of grievances, the true comedian refuses to pay attention to it and concentrates on other matters, assisting the process, if need be, by first turning on the grievance the skill in mockery he has already developed in treating less tender subjects. Pity for others is a much more difficult matter and calls for much more complex strategies of control because one dare not shun the emotion. An artist or any other person who does not feel and act on pity for the suffering of others is monstrous and all of his works will show it. Yet pity itself is a sponge, soaking up all of the other emotions. Uncontrolled it will leave its possessor despairing, without hope for a world in which suffering abounds, or it will turn him into a fanatic, sacrificing all of the playful amenities to the cause of relieving his anguish. One needs a cutoff valve that will let one feel the emotion just so long and act just so far on it, no longer and no farther.

In private life when the pity is not too urgent and one is under relatively little pressure to elaborate a rationale for abandoning it, common sense can usually be counted on to supply the cutoff. Thus Emma Woodhouse instructs her sentimental little friend Harriet, "If we feel for the wretched, enough to do all we can for them, the rest is empty sympathy, only distressing to ourselves." Though she goes on to make high, astringent comedy over the excessive complacency with which her heroine states this doctrine, Austen never contradicts it; she knows how essential it is.

But in public, political life commonsensical responses are harder to come by and defend. There the suffering that one must confront is more likely to be man-made than natural, the product of social injustice rather than natural calamities, and one has to feel some degree of responsibility for it, or at least for correcting it. Where is the

THE COMIC VISION IN LITERATURE

cutoff valve for such responsibility? How does one decide that one has gone far enough in an effort to correct the injustice? One ought to feel heavy pressure for a rationale for decisions on public, political matters. What rationale does one give or accept? And how much can you trust that or any other rationale?

Turn the issue around, concentrate on what arouses the emotion rather than on the emotion itself, and you find yourself looking at a very wide range of situations all of which are characterized by a painful discrepancy between deserts and consequences—that is, you are studying injustice and finding it everywhere. Now the question becomes how can you make, or savor, comedy in a world like *this?* Every true comedian deals with that question; each works out his own answer. None pretends that injustice is either rare or evanescent; in one way or another all accept injustice as the price of life and are willing to try to pay the price. Paradoxical as it may seem, one effect of the comic vision is to keep its possessor deeply aware of the reality of injustice. You make or savor comedy in a world like this precisely because it is a world like this.

For a clear first look at how comedy accepts injustice or at least adjusts to its inevitability we can turn to some comedies about war. War is the most spectacular source of injustice. It does not have to be a big war or a "bad" war, any war will supply it in abundance, and it does not make any difference if one is looking at it from the winning or the losing side. All war involves the slaughter of the innocent, and that is the essence of injustice. Nevertheless, complete, consistent pacifism is a position that comedy rejects for reasons that George Orwell explains in his essay on Mahatma Gandhi. (For the moment I simply assert that Orwell's vision is comic; I will justify the assertion later in this chapter.)

Gandhi's pacifism was complete. In 1938 he expressed the opinion that German Jews ought to commit collective suicide in order to arouse the world and the people of Germany to Hitler's violence, and in 1942 he urged nonviolent resistance to a seemingly imminent Japanese invasion while admitting that it might cost several million deaths. He opposed killing of all sort, even the killing of a chicken to make a broth to feed a sick child. In "Reflections on Gandhi" (*Collected Essays, Journalism, and Letters*, vol. 4) Orwell states the comic counterposition with memorable clarity:

> There must, Gandhi says, be some limit to what we will do in order to remain alive, and the limit is well on this side of chicken broth. This attitude is perhaps a noble one, but, in the sense which—I think—most people would give to the word, it is inhuman. The essence of being human is that one does not seek perfection, that one *is* sometimes willing to commit sins for the sake of loyalty, that one does not push asceticism to the point where it makes friendly intercourse impossible, and that one is prepared in the end to be defeated and broken up by life, which is the inevitable price of fastening one's love upon other human individuals. No doubt alcohol, tobacco and so forth are things that a saint must avoid, but sainthood is also a thing that human beings must avoid. (P. 527)

The comic vision does not permit a thoroughly consistent pacifism like Gandhi's because it is grounded in principles. Principles come into conflict with human needs by demanding a univocal perfectionism; comedians must remain loyal to that rock-bottom reality in which stomach, bladder, and all of the other organs take precedence over abstract ideas. Henry Miller came as close to complete pacifism as a comedian can, but as he was careful to show, his pacifism was grounded not so much in principle as in a perception that violence like greed is insatiable and in a deep disgust with modern society, which he thought would inevitably smash itself to pieces. He refused to fight to stave off the inevitable; but he also refused to fight to hurry it on, even though he saw that smashup as a necessary first step toward the building of a decent society. Anarchism made sense to Miller, but he refused to waste his life on that or any other cause.

Jaroslav Hašek was an anarchist, at least he called himself one during his years of political activity in the decade before World War I. But the hero of his great comedy about war, *The Good Soldier Švejk,* is not an anarchist; he is simply, irredeemably Švejk, an unrebellious, even uncomplaining Czech soldier in the army of the Austro-Hungarian Empire in World War I who by means of an "idiocy" that is too inspired to be natural and too consistent to be artificial renders perfectly ridiculous the whole bundle of notions that produce the concept of a "good soldier." It is lamentable that nearly all Americans must peer at Švejk through the haze of a translation, but fortunately for us there is a relatively new translation by Sir Cecil Parrott that is a vast improvement on its only predecessor. My Czech-speaking friends tell me that it still does not do justice to the dazzling vulgarity of Hašek's humor, perhaps because, as Parrott acknowledges in his introduction, it is virtually impossible to render into English the language in which Švejk expresses himself, "*common* Czech, which is not quite the same as *literary* or *book* Czech." Nonetheless, we are all indebted to Parrott. Unlike his predecessor he does not abridge the book and deliberately bowdlerize it, and he makes it possible for us to see Švejk clearly enough to understand why Czechs rate him among the great comic figures in literature.

Švejk embodies the central comic response to a world in which war is normal. He does not rebel against it—how can you rebel against an entire world? Nor does he practice nonviolent resistance, at least not of a sort that Gandhi would recognize. Given an order, he obeys eagerly, even zealously, but somehow always in such a fashion as to snarl the purposes of the authorities giving the order. Ordered to report for induction, Švejk reports, even though a few years earlier he had been discharged from the army as "a patent idiot" and even though he is suffering a crippling attack of rheumatism. Donning an army cap and wearing the gay flowers of a recruit in his buttonhole, he has his landlady trundle him through the streets of Prague in a wheelchair while he waves his crutches and shouts, "To Belgrade, to Belgrade!" This draws such a crowd that the mounted police have to escort him to the induction center—where he is promptly incarcerated on suspicion of malingering. Ordered to show respect to officers, Private Švejk exasperates his long-suffering Lieutenant Lukas by prefacing nearly every statement he makes to him with "Humbly report, sir." Ordered to walk all night to the city where his regiment is stationed after he has been accidentally left behind at a train station in a village, Švejk walks; however, leaving the village he turns west instead of south and it takes him days, not hours, to catch up with his regiment. If patriotism is called for, Švejk loudly cries, "Long live our Emperor, Franz Joseph the First" whenever he sees a picture of His Imperial Majesty, though one time he does it when he is ushered before a medical commission that is to examine his intelligence, thereby convincing them of his idiocy, and another time when he is being escorted through a crowded street by two armed guards, thereby nearly precipitating a riot. After that second incident some officers want to convict him of treason on the ground that he had been deliberately, subversively ironic.

But Švejk is never ironic. He is no Socratic wiseman playing the part of a fool in order to reveal the foolishness of common thought; wide-eyed and moon-faced, he *is* a fool, in private as well as in public. In the very first chapter, be responds to the news of the assassination at Sarajevo by saying "War is certain. Serbia and Russia will help us in it. There won't half be a blood bath." Hašek adds a descriptive comment: "Švejk looked beautiful in this prophetic moment. His simple face, smiling like a full moon, beamed with enthusiasm. Everything was so clear to him" (p. 12). There is nothing in any of the other twenty-six chapters of this long, not quite finished book (Hašek died before he could complete the fourth part) to contradict or qualify that beaming enthusiasm. Yet Švejk so steadily illuminates—as a large, well-polished, carefully aimed reflector illuminates—the stupidity of the brutal, pompous people running his army and his society that one cannot think of him as a peculiarly blessed idiot. In particular, the long, rambling anecdotes that he spills out at every possible opportunity so consistently turn out to be to the point, though they always seem to be wholly inappropriate, that one has to sense and admire an intelligence within him. Perhaps we can think of him as a man wise enough and calm enough to realize that the only way to survive in a world saturated in stupidity is to be certifiably idiotic. Do not play the fool, be the fool! Švejk is one, brilliantly.

It is not surprising that no other extensively developed character in literature embodies the comic response to war as purely as Švejk

THE COMIC VISION IN LITERATURE

does. Good fiction is always in some degree autobiographical. To create a Švejk one must have a lot of Švejk within himself and have had a lot of Švejkian experience, yet one must also have the intelligence and the drive to be a writer. That is a murderously contradictory set of requirements. Hašek, who was born in 1883, wasted his energies before the war in bohemian dissipation and in prankish political action. During the war he lived the military experiences that he used, often quite directly, as the basis for his book; he was saved from the slaughter by being captured by the Russians, an arduous and hazardous salvation. In Russia during the Revolution he was swept into politics, so seriously that he stayed sober for thirty months. But when he finally returned to Czechoslovakia late in 1920, he promptly slipped back into his old dissipation and it killed him, but not before he managed to pull out of himself in 1921 and 1922 most of *The Good Soldier Švejk*. He died in January 1923, not quite forty years old.

It is much more common for literature to focus on characters who learn how to be fools by emulating natural fools whose sweetness and wisdom they have come to admire. A good example would be the "I" of E. E. Cummings's autobiographical book *The Enormous Room* (1922). Cummings was a well-educated young man and poet who was already starting to develop his own distinctive version of transcendental beliefs when he was snatched out of the Norton-Harjes Ambulance Corps in October 1917 and thrown into the French concentration camp at La Ferté Macé, where he shared a corner of a barracks with some fools who were classified as "scum" by the authorities and as "Delectable Mountains" by Cummings. Naturally, inevitably, the foolishness which the "I" of his book embodies is both learned and learn-ed, far closer to the foolishness of a Thoreau than to that of a Švejk.

A more typical and fictional example of the hero who learns his foolishness in time of war is Yossarian in Heller's *Catch-22*. Yossarian struggles all through the novel to master the foolishness that comes naturally to his friend Orr. As his name suggests, Orr realizes that there is an alternative to flying bombing mission after bombing mission until you are killed; you can work as hard to save your life as others do to lose theirs. Orr, in contrast to most of the other pilots, navigators, and bombardiers of the 256th Bomber Squadron, is decidedly not middle class; he is a tinkerer, a man whose one economically useful gift is the ability to repair or devise intricate mechanisms—in other words, a man who could be classified in modern society as downwardly mobile. He applies his gift to his problem and arrives at a solution: he practices crash landings until the time is right to desert; then, he crashes in the Mediterranean, waits until his crew heads toward shore and "safety," and sets off in the plane's other inflatable boat toward the open sea, determined to row to Sweden, where he can sit out the rest of the war as an internee.

Orr's "foolishness" lies in the calm, unthinking completeness with which he accepts the fact that he is an individual, a single, necessarily self-sufficient integer, not a statistic, not a component of a social mass. He is Orr, buck-toothed, apple-cheeked, and stupid-looking. If he does not preserve himself, nobody else will, and the individual self is worth preserving. Yossarian has to work hard to reach that understanding. He has, at least at first, most of the middle-class virtues; he is educated, articulate, responsible, and ambitious. He is the best bombardier in the squadron and by the time he rebels he has flown more than sixty combat missions. He is saved from himself—or for himself—first by his love of women. He loves them for the sexual pleasure they give him, but also he loves them because they are feminine and not caught in the web of ideas and attitudes that make armies possible. Second, he has a saving capacity for paranoia. Everybody, he slowly realizes, is out to kill him, the Germans by shooting his plane down, the Americans by sending him where he will get shot down. Third, and most important, he goes to the assistance of a gunner named Snowdon who had been wounded by flak and thereby learns his "secret." Snowdon's secret, revealed when Yossarian rips open the snaps of his flak jacket and "whole mottled quarts" of his insides slither onto the floor of the plane, is that "man was matter. . . . Drop him out a window and he'll fall. Set fire to

him and he'll burn. Bury him and he'll rot, like other kinds of garbage. The spirit gone, man is garbage. That was Snowdon's secret.
Ripeness is all'' (pp. 457–58).

Still, it takes the news that Orr has been washed ashore in Sweden
after weeks at sea to push Yossarian to decisive action—to run away
to Sweden. Even then he explains himself as no real fool would:
"I'm not running *away* from my responsibilities. I'm running *to*
them. There's nothing negative about running away to save my life"
(p. 469). A real fool does not believe in explanations. That is why
Orr would never tell Yossarian what he was up to; he simply suggested that he request assignment to his crew. Yossarian was afraid
to fly with him, even though Orr pointed out that nobody had ever
been hurt flying with him. Yossarian was too intelligent to take his
chances with a fool, however much he liked him, too smart to figure
out what any fool could understand until it was all acted out for him.

Like Cummings, Heller is too literate, too well educated (degrees
from New York University and Columbia, Fulbright study at Ox-
ford, teaching at Pennsylvania State) to have a natural fool within
him. He not only knows Shakespeare—"Ripeness is all"—but he
has also studied Joyce and picked up on Eliot's remarks (in his essay
on Marlowe) about the possibility of a "serious, even savage" kind
of farce. Mixing ideas of structure learned from Joyce with jokes
borrowed from the lowest sources of American humor—burlesque
theaters, slapstick films, movie cartoons, and joke-books—Heller
creates a very serious, certainly savage farce about war. Yossarian's
friends die in bizarre ways. Clevenger flies into a cloud and never
emerges from it, Kid Sampson stands up on a raft and is cut in half
by the propeller on a plane that is buzzing the beach, Hungry Joe
smothers in his sleep when a cat curls up on his face, and Dunbar
simply "is disappeared." But nearly all of them do die. Because of
the scrambled chronology of the novel we learn of many of the
deaths long before they are dramatized and find characters in scenes
long after their deaths have been fully described. Snowdon's death
"occurs" many times throughout the book, though it is not until the
end that his "secret" is formally stated. The result is a potent meaningful confusion; at any given point we cannot be sure who "really"

is alive and we are hard put to give a rational explanation for many of the deaths that we think have occurred. Heller forces us to realize that most of these men are as good as dead as soon as they start flying combat missions, which is to say, as soon as the slaughter begins, and to agree that an account of a slaughter has no business being clear, coherent, and reasonable.

The hero of Thomas Berger's comedy about war, *Little Big Man*, is less a fool than a prankster, and more a drifter than either. During the years of sporadic fighting between Indians and white men that culminated in the Battle of Little Big Horn he drifts back and forth across the frontier living sometimes as a white man known as Jack Crabb and sometimes as a Cheyenne Indian known as Little Big Man. Both of his lives provide him with a full experience of violence and of the injustice it creates; his problem is to survive and to do so without going crazy.

Jack lives with the white men until he is about nine, when his father, a crackpot preacher who thinks that Indians are descendants of the lost tribe of Israel, precipitates the slaughter of all of the men in their small wagon train by giving a jug of whiskey to a band of Cheyenne braves. Jack winds up, through a series of comic misunderstandings, living with the Cheyenne. He flourishes as a Cheyenne even gaining renown, through more comic misunderstandings, as a warrior—until he gets trapped in a white raid on the Indians' camp and saves himself by persuading a thickheaded soldier that he really is white. From then on he bounces back and forth between his two identities, pushed each time by an act of violence, until finally, after the Battle of the Washita where forces under the command of General Custer destroyed a large Indian encampment, he decides to remain white because he cannot stand to be on the losing side of any more massacres. Sure enough, that decision brings Jack to Little Big Horn; he is the sole survivor of "Custer's Last Stand," rescued by his only true enemy among the Cheyenne, a fierce brave whose sole purpose in saving him was to repay an old debt and thereby make it possible for him to kill Jack at some later time without losing his honor.

A life like that is enough to drive any man insane, if it does not kill him first, but Jack survives with most of his odd faculties intact to narrate, at age 111, his story through his last experience as Little Big Man. He witnesses the death of Old Lodge Skins, his Cheyenne father, who has decided that his time has come; the old chief simply stops living, but before he does he explains to Jack that it does not make any difference whether he is white or Indian, a survivor or a victim, because "we are all men together." Jack's long survival can be credited to his having the great good luck and the stubborn attachment to life that characterize all of comedy's survivors. His sanity is a more complex matter.

At the heart of it is his capacity for something like the analogical thinking that Lynch celebrates; that is, he is able to perceive the similarities between ways of thinking and living as dissimilar as the Cheyenne and the white ways while still perceiving and even appreciating their differences. The Cheyenne way is circular; the white way linear. The Cheyenne see themselves as living in a circle of being where they have well-defined functions and an obligation to respect the way things are; the whites see themselves as living in a line of history where they have, or should have, distinct purposes and an obligation to change things to the way they should be. The Cheyenne live in round, movable lodges, avoid straight-ahead movements either in travel or in argument, disturb the earth as little as possible, and have a glorious time fighting with other tribes. The whites live in square houses built on solid foundations, love the notion and the feeling of forging ahead come hell or high water, serve purposes that they are likely to describe as ideals, are remarkably ingenious in discovering ways to alter the earth to suit those purposes, and profess to hate fighting, though they can be murderously efficient at it. Yet Jack finds similarities within the differences. If the whites assign ladies the task of embodying some of their more preposterous ideals while leaving men free to do the dirty work, the Cheyenne assign women the dreary tasks necessary to daily life while leaving men free to carry on the noble work of hunting and fighting. If the Cheyenne have their "contraries"—warriors so devoted to fighting that they do everything not connected with fighting backward—the whites have their gunfighters—men like Wild Bill Hickock, whose every waking moment is devoted to refining the skills that permit him to shoot other men before they can shoot him. If whites use arguments and military discipline to keep you in line, the Cheyenne use legends and fear of shame to get the same results. And if Jack Crabb loses his white wife and child to an Indian raiding party, Little Big Man loses his Indian wife and child to Custer's regiment. White hostility may be more generalized and more broadly destructive than Cheyenne hostility, but you are just as dead whether you are killed by an arrow from an ancient bow or a bullet from a modern rifle.

Thus, Jack can understand Old Lodge Skins' message that "we were all men together" to mean that neither white nor Indian has any special claim on either blame or glory; in neither of his identities does he himself need to feel either guilt or pride. Nor does he need to feel shame because he has finally chosen to live a white life. The Cheyenne way of life is, as both Jack and Old Lodge Skins recognize, finished. A circular way of life cannot exist alongside a linear one; neither would nor could tolerate the other. To put it in textbook terms, a primitive, pretechnological society cannot exist alongside a civilized, technological society; each must intrude on the space the other requires. The linear culture will always win the resultant conflict, and not simply because it has better weapons and a stronger will to conquer. As Jack's friend Lavender, a former slave who has lived with the Sioux for a number of years, puts it the night before they both ride with Custer to his last stand, "If you come from civilization to live among the savages, it is fine for a while and then you get so powerful curious as to what is going on back home, you can't stand it. You got to see, so you come back, and it might be good or it might be awful, but it is happening" (p. 371). The linear culture's promise that something might *happen* tomorrow is more potent, more addictive than anything the circular culture can offer.

By accepting violence and injustice in the way that he does, Jack frees himself to live in history without feeling the twin compulsions toward guilt and resentment that make so much of human history appalling. If we must remember ourselves as either winners or losers then our future can be no better than our past, but if we can learn something like Jack's comic remembrance of a past in which we were simply all men together then there is some hope for the future. With a comic remembrance we can hope to bend a linear culture enough to give it a saving degree of circularity.

Heinrich Böll, to cite one last example, has struggled to reach essentially the same kind of comic remembrance; though as a German who had to fight in World War II for a cause he despised, he has found the struggle hard and the comedy that has emerged from it is far more astringent than Berger's. His major works on the theme of the war, *Billiards at Half-Past Nine* (1962) and *Group Portrait with Lady* (1971), are much too complex for quick discussion; I will simply point out that the two novellas published in this country under the title *Absent without Leave* support, sometimes quite precisely, the ideas of the other books I have discussed in this section. Wilhelm Schmölder, the narrator of the title novella, "Absent without Leave," is as one with Švejk, though like Cummings's "I" and Heller's Yossarian he has had to learn his "celestial common sense" from another: "You become human when you go absent without leave from your unit: I found this out, and offer it as candid advice to later generations. (But watch out when they start shooting! There are some idiots who aim to hit!)" (p. 73). The unnamed narrator of the second novella, "Enter and Exit," shares with Yossarian and Jack Crabb a conviction of the murderous consequences of univocal logic and even more strongly than Yossarian does, he associates it with masculinity. One of the logicians among his fellow prisoners of war, he says, had "tried to drum up a kind of court of honor that was to deny me the quality of being German (and I had wished that this court, which never convened, had actually had the power to deny me this quality). What they didn't know was that I hated them, Nazis and non-Nazis, not because of their political views but because they were men, men of the same species as those I had to spend the last six years with; the words man and stupid had become almost identical for me" (pp. 125–26).

Švejk, Yossarian, and Jack Crabb are all almost perfectly apolitical; they cannot afford to be otherwise. In this respect, as in others, they are like Huck Finn, who is too weak and vulnerable himself to be able to give any thought to improving the violent and unjust society he finds himself in. Huck's response to his society is the central comic response to all societies: Don't take stands; keep moving. If you must take a stand—"All right, then, I'll *go* to hell!"—take it shiftily and go to hell as ingloriously as possible. But it is much better to keep moving. Light out for the Territory. If there is no open territory at the geographical edge of your society, head for one of those inner "territories" that exist in every society, usually near the bottom of the heap. Henry Miller, after all, found a perfectly usable territory right in the gutters of New York and Paris.

But not all comedians can play the apolitical part of a Huck Finn or a Henry Miller. Some are trapped—by temperament, training, and circumstance—in a necessity for political thought and action. Böll, who like his fictional heroes cannot convene a court that can deprive him of the quality of being German, is a good example and his solution is probably typical. He does not so much keep moving as keep his distance, and in novels like *End of a Mission* (1968) and *The Lost Honor of Katherina Blum* (1974) he comments sardonically on the stupid injustices of a society he has no intention of abandoning. Or one could take two of Isben's heroes as nicely bracketing the common range of possibilities, Dr. Stockmann in *An Enemy of the People* and Relling in *The Wild Duck*.

Unlike most comic heroes, Dr. Stockmann is an intellectual, but he is similar to Quixote. He is decent enough to want justice for all, naive enough to think that he can get his townspeople to see the error of their ways, and "mad" enough to be wholly unaffected by greed. Though *An Enemy of the People* is often treated as if it were a melodrama for liberals, Dr. Stockmann's conclusions are comic: "You should never wear your best trousers when you go out to fight for truth and freedom!" "I just want to din into the heads of these poor misguided mongrels, that party programs do nothing but stifle living truths—that justice and morality are being turned upside down by expediency and greed—until eventually life itself will scarcely be worth living! Surely I ought to be able to make the people see that, Captain Horster? Don't you think so?'' And finally, ''I've made a great discovery. . . . The strongest man in the world is the man who stands alone.'' (All quotes are from *Six Plays,* act 5.) Of course, when he states his great discovery he is surrounded by two young sons (who are well on their way to becoming carbon copies of him), an absolutely adoring daughter, and a ruefully loving wife.

Relling is also an intellectual observer of society, but where Dr. Stockmann is sunny and energetic he is somber and all but defeated; the comedy of *The Wild Duck* has a harsh, metallic taste. Relling, who describes himself as ''a doctor of sorts,'' treats Hjalmar Ekdal as he treats all of his patients, by feeding ''the life-lie in him''—that is, by nurturing an illusion that will keep the poor fool going, in Ekdal's case the illusion that he is destined to invent something that will revolutionize photography. Relling sees the words *ideals* and *lies* as synonyms, about as closely related ''as typhus and putrid fever''; his antagonist is Gregers Werle, who presses ''the claim of the ideal'' on Ekdal and everyone else who will listen to him. Nothing, not Relling's sardonic arguments, not even Hedwig's pathetic suicide, can cure Gregers of his posturing. The play ends this way (Michael Meyer's translation):

> RELLING: Oh, life would be all right if we didn't have to put up with these damned creditors who keep pestering us with the demands of their ideals.
> GREGERS: (*Stares ahead of him*) In that case, I am glad that my destiny is what it is.
> RELLING: And what, if I may ask, is your destiny.
> GREGERS: (*As he goes towards the door*) To be the thirteenth at the table.
> (*Relling laughs and spits.*)

Ibsen did not work out a coherent political position; ''his iron humor,'' which George Bernard Shaw identified and admired, carried him in other directions toward different tasks. In the twentieth century two writers have made particularly heroic efforts to be politically active and effective while remaining faithful to a comic vision of reality, George Orwell (1903–1950) and Ignazio Silone (1900–1978). Though they started from very different beginnings— Orwell as a graduate of Eton serving for five years in the Indian Imperial Police; Silone as a graduate of a Catholic school in the Abruzzi district of Italy serving for thirteen years in first socialist then communist revolutionary political parties in Italy and throughout Europe—they reached similar conclusions. Both were vividly aware of social injustice and stubbornly insistent on making others equally aware of it. Both recognized that organized revolutionary activity always has been and probably always will be a trap beautifully designed to destroy the values in the name of which revolutions are made; yet neither would tamely submit to the status quo. Similarly, both brought religious values to bear on political concerns, yet neither had faith in any church. Orwell was so deeply embedded in an English Protestant tradition that he could not conceive of a Catholic being free enough to write a good novel, and Silone was so much an Italian Catholic that his imagination derived nearly all of its symbolic gestures from the rituals of the Church. Thus, there was an important difference in their final similarity. Both demanded that politics respect the freedom and dignity of the individual; but the Protestant Orwell asked for decency in political thought and action, and the Catholic Silone asked for a politics built on a respect for the sacramental quality of any kind of communion between individuals.

Silone's ideas and vision were best expressed in his novel *Bread and Wine*—in the original version published in 1937, not in the revised version that he published in 1955 and that was translated into English in 1962. The original is a great, rough, almost jagged work of art; the revision is only a thoughtful, interesting, skillful work of competence. The ideas and vision of the man who was born Eric Blair are best expressed in the essays in which he created the writer George Orwell. This is not to deny value to the numerous other works of both writers—that would be silly—but *Bread and Wine* and the best of the essays render with extraordinary integrity Silone's and

Orwell's senses of a reality that is so contradictory that one must simultaneously accept it as sacred and rebel against it as corrupt. Indeed, their integrity is so powerful as to render the customary techniques of critical analysis repulsive; one would like to respond to them simply by quoting whole scenes, most of which are in effect parables, from the novel and whole paragraphs from the essays. Unfortunately—or perhaps fortunately—I do not have space here to employ that appropriately humble nontechnique.

Brutally oversimplifying, then, *Bread and Wine* confronts its hero and its reader with three truths which it makes inescapably clear: that conventional, party-structured revolutions are futile, simply replacing one tyranny with another; that a Fascist state is intolerable; and that "one has only what one gives." Each truth is shown in a variety of ways, frequently with remarkable concreteness.

Bread and Wine begins with its hero, Pietro Spina, realizing the futility of the revolutionary activity that has forced him to live in exile for the past ten years, but he cannot admit that he realizes it, not even to himself. All he realizes is that he must come back to Italy, to his own place and people, no matter that he is very sick with tuberculosis and that the Fascist police are anxious to arrest him. Bit by bit his experience living disguised as the priest Don Paolo Spada forces him to full awareness of the abstractness and sterility of what he has thought and done as a revolutionary. It has all been beside the point; he has been trying to arouse the oppressed peasants with words. But because they are truly oppressed people and have been under a variety of regimes for centuries, they are not susceptible to words; they submit only to facts. "The facts of dictatorship must be confronted, not with the words of liberty, but with the facts of liberty" (p. 130). Yet a man serving a revolutionary party is not free to be such a fact. What he learns in the mountains as Spada, he learns again in Rome as Spina when he visits his friend and fellow party member Uliva. Uliva is lost in despair. He has realized that any party, perhaps especially a revolutionary party, must have its orthodoxy; yet orthodoxy breeds bureaucracy, and bureaucracy enforces tyranny. "I read and studied in my privations, and sought for at least a prom-

COMEDY AND INJUSTICE

ise of liberation. . . . I found none. Every revolution, every single one, without any exception whatever, started as a movement for liberation and finished as a tyranny'' (p. 175). Two days later Uliva, his pregnant wife, and the lodgers in the flat below are killed by the premature explosion of a bomb that he was preparing in order to blow up a church during a visit by government dignitaries.

That a Fascist state is intolerable is a lesson no sane man who has ever had a taste of freedom needs to be taught; certainly Spina does not. Yet Spina, and the reader who has been fortunate enough to live at some remove from Fascism, needs to learn, repeatedly, how pervasive, how disgusting, how ridiculous the Fascist state really is. It corrupts everybody it touches, and it touches nearly everyone, making it impossible for individuals to be honest with their parents, their children, their lovers, their friends, and least of all with themselves. The better educated and more ambitious a person is the more surely it corrupts him. Those who are least corrupted by the state are the poor, especially the poor peasants. For them it is at best irrelevant, at worst just another burden in their lives that are already fearfully overburdened in a struggle for mere survival. The ridiculousness of the state is summarized, as most things are in this book, in a symbolic action—the country-people, who have been forced to gather in the town square to listen to a broadcast of Il Duce's declaration of war against Ethiopia, chanting CHAY DOO! CHAY DOO! throughout the speech (pp. 202-3). But the evil of the state is equally well summarized—in the murders of a saintly priest, Don Benedetto, and a one-time informer, Luigi Murica. The Fascists murder the one by poisoning the wine with which he is to celebrate a mass; the other, they kill with clownish brutality:

> He had written on a piece of paper: ''Truth and brotherhood will reign among men in the place of hatred and deceit; living labor will reign in the place of money.'' When they arrested him they found that piece of paper on him, and he didn't disown it. So they put a chamberpot on his head instead of a crown, in the yard of the militia barracks at Fossa. ''That is the truth,'' they told him. They put a broom in his right hand instead of a scepter. ''That is brotherhood,'' they told him. Then they

wrapped his body in a red carpet they picked up from the floor. They
bound him, and the soldiers kicked and punched him backwards and
forwards among themselves. "That is living labor," they told him.
When he fell they walked on him, trampling on him with their nailed
boots. That was how the judicial investigation began. He survived it
for two days. (P. 309)

Silone perceived the evil of Fascism as Arendt did in *Eichmann in
Jerusalem* as banal—or better, because he too is an artist rather than
a critic, as Faulkner perceived the evil he dealt with in his stories and
novels as fifth-rate. From top to bottom, from "Etcetera, Etcetera,"
the ineffable leader, down to the merest hangers-on, Silone's Fascists are so many bad jokes (like Percy Grimm in *Light in August*),
more likely to induce vomiting than laughter; but the people that they
oppress are (like Byron Bunch and Lena Grove) genuinely, unconsciously humorous, repeatedly the occasion for deep, true laughter.
The funniest extended scene in the novel, which is shot full of funny
incidents and observations, takes place in Rome, where the Fascist
presence is strongest. It is the account of a confidence scheme
worked on Nordic lady tourists by two of Spina's impoverished
countrymen, Achilles Scarpa and Managgia Lamorra; Lamorra,
playing the part of "The Monster Outside the Gates," accosts them,
and Achilles rescues them. There are three faults in the scheme:
some of the ladies succumb to the Monster before Achilles can rescue them; when the rescue proceeds on schedule the two men get so
carried away with their roles that they batter and bruise each other
mercilessly; and finally, the rescued ladies are so anxious to repay
Achilles with sexual favors that his manly pride forbids him to take
money from them, too, even though the money was the object of the
whole scheme. This scene is in the same chapter as the accounts of
Uliva's despair and death and the rape of Luigi Murica's girl by two
Fascist policemen (pp. 160–91).

Bread and Wine's third truth, that "one has only what one gives,"
is the sternest and most complex of all. It is what emerges from
almost every incident in the book; as Spina's understanding of it
deepens, layer by layer, he falls further and further away from the

slogans and abstractions of his party past. He finally realizes that he can neither move others to revolutionary action nor recover a self that he can stand to live with until he enters a true communion with others. The realization is expressed in symbolic action when as Don Paolo he hears Luigi Murica's confession of his past as a police informer and replies by putting his life in Murica's hands: "I am not a priest, and Don Paolo Spada is not my real name. My real name is Pietro Spina." The great, fundamental revolutionary act is to tell the truth, simply and openly. One has only what one gives, and if one does not give truth all that one has must be false. But that is a stern doctrine, for it sends Murica to his death behind the militia barracks. It also sends, at the very end of the novel, a girl named Cristina to her death in a snowy mountain pass, where she has gone to help Spina escape from the Fascists; she is caught by a pack of hungry wolves that otherwise would have fed on Spina.

That is a grim ending for a comedy, but Italy in the 1930s was a grim place for a comedian to be—or rather, to imagine himself being, for Silone was living and writing in exile, across the border in Switzerland. There was a similar load of grimness in Orwell's work; there had to be. In the twenties, during his stint as a police officer in Burma, he participated in the mean-spirited oppression of imperialism; in the early thirties, he lived with the down and out in Paris, London, and other places, learning at first hand the suffering with which those at the bottom of the heap of capitalism pay for the comforts of those at the top of the heap. In 1937 he went to Spain to fight Fascism and discovered there the evil of left-wing totalitarianism, too; he was wounded at the front in May and had to flee the Republic in June because the communists had declared illegal the small party in whose brigade he had fought. In 1939 came the war with all of its horrors, though to his disgust Orwell was rejected for military duty by the doctors. In the few years left to him after the war—he died of tuberculosis in January 1950—Orwell saw very clearly the nature of cold war politics. There is a lot of reason for grimness in that personal history, yet almost all of his writing shows, usually plainly, that it is the product of an essentially comic vision. The one major exception is *Nineteen Eighty-Four,* which he wrote in 1947–1948 when his illness was becoming increasingly severe and when he felt the urgency of shocking us into an awareness of what our political policies were leading us toward. The huge popularity of that despairing book has made it difficult for many people to see the real nature of Orwell's position.

A good place to start toward a better understanding of him is the essay "Why I Write." (Though it was written in 1946, the editors of his *Collected Essays, Journalism and Letters* have placed it at the beginning of the first of the four chronologically arranged volumes as an appropriate introduction to the whole set.) He asserts that there are four great motives for writing prose: sheer egoism, aesthetic enthusiasm, historical impulse, and political purpose. He thinks that in a more peaceful age he might have written "ornate or merely descriptive books," but in "an age like this" a writer must embrace political purpose. "Every line of serious work that I have written since 1936 has been written, directly or indirectly, *against* totalitarianism and *for* democratic socialism, as I understand it." (Nearly the same could be said for the writing he did before 1936, too; he was never apolitical.) Yet he has remained loyal to his aesthetic motive as well, trying to make political writing into an art. Even when he writes "downright propaganda," he must include things that "a full-time politician would consider irrelevant." Then he adds a credo that could come only from a comic artist: "I am not able, and I do not want, completely to abandon the world-view that I acquired in childhood. So long as I remain alive and well I shall continue to feel strongly about prose style, to love the surface of the earth, and to take a pleasure in solid objects and scraps of useless information" (vol. 1, pp. 25–28).

There is the central quality in Orwell's best work, the source of the distinctive "sound" of his prose: tension between political and aesthetic motives, a double pull between an obligation to further the cause of democratic socialism and a fidelity to "childish" loves of language and nature, of solid objects and useless information. Or, to put it in terms appropriate to this book, he will at the same time serve a purpose and honor purposelessness. His most forceful political pieces not only include but hinge on things that full-time politicians and propagandists would ignore, while his essays on seemingly non-political subjects derive their power from his dedication to his political cause.

Animal Farm is an allegory on the perversion of the Russian Revolution by Stalin, but it is also a fable for children derived from the commonplace experience of seeing "a little boy, perhaps ten years old, driving a huge cart-horse along a narrow path" ("Author's Preface to the Ukrainian Edition of *Animal Farm*," vol. 3, p. 458). "Shooting an Elephant" is a penetrating analysis of imperialism precisely because it is so open to a childlike delight in animals and a childish fear of being laughed at. Shooting that elephant while he is "beating his bunch of grass against his knees with that preoccupied grandmotherly air that elephants have," simply because a crowd of Burmese will laugh at him if he does not, enables Orwell to reach directly to the central, crucial objection to all forms of imperialism and tyranny: "I perceived in this moment that when the white man turns tyrant it is his own freedom that he destroys" (vol. 1, pp. 269–70). And the elephant's slow death while he fired shot after shot into it gives him a perfect symbolic expression of the ghastly irrelevance of tyranny: "He was dying, very slowly and in great agony, but in some world remote from me where not even a bullet could damage him further" (vol. 1, p. 272). Similarly, the experience of having an Arab who is employed by the municipality ask for a piece of the bread he is feeding to a gazelle in the public gardens gives him in "Marrakech" a way of measuring the exploitiveness of French imperialism that anyone can understand. And Orwell could come to the defense of P. G. Wodehouse when others were piously denouncing him as a collaborator—for having made some broadcasts over Berlin radio while he was interned in Germany—in large part because he had started reading Wodehouse when he was about eight years old and he remained loyal to the pleasure Wodehouse had given him. Also, Orwell understood just how idiotically free of political awareness Wodehouse's work is ("In Defence of P. G. Wodehouse").

To see the double pull from the other side one can look at "Boys'

Weeklies,'' where his awareness of their right-wing attitudes and assumptions structures a long, yet good-humored and interested, analysis of popular magazines for boys; or at "Benefit of Clergy,'' where his concern to understand their social and political significance for those who admire them puts a cold cutting edge on his disgust for the paintings of Salvador Dali. In "Funny, But Not Vulgar,'' his political concern gives him a useful working definition of what causes laughter: "A thing is funny when—in some way that is not actually offensive or frightening—it upsets the established order'' (vol. 3, p. 325). That in turn makes possible a quick, convincing analysis of the class biases and interests that underlie genteel demands for humor that is not "vulgar.''

But to see the tension in Orwell's thought at its most richly rewarding level one should go to "Politics and the English Language'' (vol. 4, pp. 156–70), an essay that everyone who tries to think or write about English prose style now leans on. Here I must resort to pure, undecorated quotation, being careful to respect the order in which the statements occur in the essay:

> Now, it is clear that the decline of a language must ultimately have political and economic causes.

> . . . The fight against bad English is not frivolous and is not the exclusive concern of professional writers.

> This mixture of vagueness and sheer incompetence is the most marked characteristic of modern English prose, and especially of any kind of political writing. As soon as certain topics are raised, the concrete melts into the abstract and no one seems able to think of turns of speech that are not hackneyed: prose consists less and less of *words* chosen for the sake of their meaning, and more and more of *phrases* tacked together like the sections of a prefabricated hen-house.

> Here is a well-known verse from *Ecclesiastes:* "I returned and saw under the sun, that the race is not to the swift, nor the battle to the strong, neither yet bread to the wise, nor yet riches to men of understanding, nor yet favour to men of skill; but time and chance happeneth to them all.''

Here it is in modern English: "Objective consideration of contemporary phenomena compels the conclusion that success or failure in competitive activities exhibits no tendency to be commensurate with innate capacity, but that a considerable element of the unpredictable must invariably be taken into account."

In our time, political speech and writing are largely the defence of the indefensible.

It [the defense of the English language] has nothing to do with correct grammar and syntax, which are of no importance so long as one makes one's meaning clear, or with the avoidance of Americanisms, or with having what is called a "good prose style."

If you simplify your English, you are freed from the worst follies of orthodoxy. You cannot speak any of the necessary dialects, and when you make a stupid remark its stupidity will be obvious, even to yourself.

Orwell's emphasis on the reciprocal relation between politics (taking that term as broadly as possible) and language is crucial to nearly all of his work, not just this one essay. It leads to or is the product of—there is no determining which is cause and which is effect—his highest value, decency. In a world in which injustice is inevitable and in which, therefore, revolution is certain to be futile, producing only "a temporary relief, such as a sick man gets by turning over in bed" (vol. 4, p. 36), decency in all dealings with others is the highest form of political action; it is also a moral obligation and a psychic necessity. As an idea it may seem thin and simple, especially to people with any degree of intellectual sophistication, but as a guide to action it is powerful and demanding, the Protestant equivalent of Silone's Catholic ideal of a sacramental sense of communion in daily life. As a theme for art it is durable and effective. One could take as an epigraph for all of Orwell's work, perhaps especially for the four volumes of *The Collected Essays, Journalism and Letters,* a sentence that he wrote in a book review in 1936: "The fact to which we have to cling, as to a life-belt, is that it *is* possible to be a normal decent person and yet to be fully alive" (vol. 1, p. 256). The extraordinary achievement of the essays is that it is impossible to read them without believing that the "fact" is indeed a *fact*.

It is a shame that Orwell never wrote an essay about Thoreau's "On the Duty of Civil Disobedience." I imagine that Thoreau's transcendentalism would have been too abstract to suit him, and he surely would have registered the same objection to Thoreau's strategy that he did to the one Gandhi derived from it: that it would not work in a twentieth-century totalitarian state. But just as surely he would have applauded Thoreau's central doctrine: "It is not a man's duty, as a matter of course, to devote himself to the eradication of any, even the most enormous wrong; he may still properly have other concerns to engage him; but it is his duty, at least, to wash his hands of it, and, if he gives it no thought longer, not to give it practically his support." And I think he would have appreciated the rightness of Thoreau's action the morning after his famous night in jail: "I was put into jail as I was going to the shoe-maker's to get a shoe which was mended. When I was let out the next morning, I proceeded to finish my errand, and, having put on my mended shoe, joined a huckleberry party, who were impatient to put themselves under my conduct; and in half an hour,—for the horse was soon tackled,—was in the midst of a huckleberry field, on one of our highest hills, two miles off, and then the State was nowhere to be seen." Orwell lived in fear, as we all must, that we are fast approaching a time in which it will be impossible to discover a hill from which the State is nowhere to be seen, but he knew that the best party for a sane and decent man to give his loyalty to is a huckleberry party. The comic truth, which can be difficult, is that one can do nothing to preserve the world from the ravages of fanatics unless one first preserves oneself from fanaticism.

As I suggested at the beginning of this chapter, all comedians, political or apolitical, in war or in peace, must confront the reality of injustice or resign themselves to being hopelessly trivial and false. I doubt that any comic artist ever confronted that reality and the philosophical problems it creates any more systematically than Joyce Cary did. When he first decided to write novels, after the lingering effects of wounds he suffered in World War I forced him out of colonial service in Africa, he found that though he started several, including one that he thought contained some of the best writing he ever did, he could not finish any because they raised "political and religious questions" that he could not answer (*Writers at Work*, p. 63). It was not until he put himself through a "new education," which concentrated on the issues of injustice and freedom, that he was able to complete a novel. He was forty when *Aissa Saved* was published; in the twenty-five years before his death in 1957, he completed fourteen more and nearly completed a fifteenth, *The Captive and the Free*. They could all have been published under the title of an essay that he considered publishing as a general preface to the Carfax edition of his novels, "Comedy of Freedom." The reasoning that supports this title is very clearly laid out in his one book of criticism, *Art and Reality*.

Cary's key idea is one that I quoted earlier (in my discussion of Sara Monday in chapter 4): "So we have a reality consisting of permanent and highly obstinate facts, and permanent and highly obstinate human nature" (p. 19). It is the permanence and the obstinacy of facts and human nature that give them value. Bricks that could stop being bricks at will or hearts that could stop beating at will would be of no use to anyone. Moreover, the gap between the two aspects of reality—Cary is willing to label them mind and matter—is also permanent and obstinate. Mind can affect matter, at least enough to alter its shapes, and matter certainly affects minds; but finally the one is not the other, the gap is permanent. Each of us must live at some remove from the rest of reality, alone and vulnerable, but also free. The existence of that gap between what the mind wants and what matter will deliver guarantees the existence of pain, suffering, and injustice. If rocks are going to be rocks and flesh is going to be flesh, then toes will be stubbed and fingers crushed, no matter how innocent persons may be. Yet by the same token, if minds are going to be minds, men are going to be free to exercise their creative imaginations in perceiving and dealing with all of the things on the other side of the gap; men are not mosquitoes, controlled by instincts over which they have no individual power. And if men are free in and with their imaginations, they must also be free to suffer, cause, and even deliberately inflict injustice in all of its manifold forms. "The world is inescapably shot through with luck, because it is also shot through with freedom" (p. 61). Injustice is the price of freedom. Freedom is worth the price, Cary thinks; all people whose vision is comic agree, though they may not have arrived at the conclusion in the way Cary has.

Cary himself did not realize it, but Henry James was in full agreement with him. One can see that in *The Ambassadors* with its tracing of Lambert Strether's liberation by his acceptance of a world that cannot be tidied up to conform to the ideals of Woollett, Massachusetts. One can also see it in all of the short stories that F. O. Matthiessen gathered under the title *Stories of Writers and Artists* and with particular clarity in "The Next Time," which James wrote in 1895. It is the story of Ray Limbert, a novelist of rare skill who, like Henry James, makes a series of desperate attempts to write something that will be a commercial success because, unlike Henry James, he has a wife, children, and a mother-in-law to support; but the harder he tries the more deeply he fails, frustrated by "the purity of his gift." Each book in the economically disastrous procession is merely "an unscrupulous, an unsparing, a shameless merciless masterpiece" instead of the golden chunk of obvious, popular trash he was aiming for. In perfect contrast to him is his sister-in-law, Jane Highmore, "one of the most voluminous writers of the time," who cannot stop herself from producing three-volume successes for the lending libraries even though she yearns to be, just once, like Ray Limbert, "an exquisite failure." She even tries to persuade the narrator, a perceptive, dedicated critic, to write a piece in praise of one of her novels in the belief that it will have the same blighting effect on her sales that his similar pieces have had on Limbert's sales. Naturally, she will not believe the narrator's declaration that "a book sold might easily be as glorious as a book unsold"; she wants a failure and she knows that his own repeated failures make him "well qualified to place the laurel."

I will not summarize the details of this Jamesian parable of talents in the commercial world of book publishing; it is enough to say that it is a remarkably good-humored refraction of James's own struggles with "the bitch goddess" success (to use his brother's famous phrase), written less than a year after the humiliating failure of his play, *Guy Domville*. But "The Next Time" is something more than an epigrammatic working out of the implications of a three-sided joke; it is also a full, comic recognition of the harsh truth that in this world there is a grotesque disproportion between effort and results, between cause and effect. That is, like any sound parable of talents it is about injustice. There is no justice for Ray Limbert in the fact that the worst work he can do for magazine publishers is not bad enough to suit them, or in the fact that the burden of supporting his mother-in-law's expensive snobbishness falls mainly on him rather than on his bestselling sister-in-law. Nor is there any justice in his death at an early age, brought on by an English winter because he could not afford to go to Egypt. However, there is a compensation: in the last months of his life he floated away from all concern for the marketplace "into a grand indifference, into a reckless consciousness of art. . . . He had merely waked up one morning again in the country of the blue and had stayed there with a good conscience and a great idea" (p. 279). That he does not live to complete his story "Derogation" is irrelevant—just as it is irrelevant in *The Horse's Mouth* that Gulley Jimson does not live to complete "The Creation." James's point is the same as Cary's: in an unjust world one can be free to explore "the country of the blue"; that freedom is the only, but more than sufficient, compensation for injustice. James would agree with the related points that Cary makes in *Art and Reality:* that we are all willy-nilly artists, at least in some part, at least some of the time; and that though only great artists can map that country, the rest of us can learn its geography by studying what they have done.

It is surprising that Cary tends to misunderstand James. He sees James as focusing on the tragic "fragility of all goodness, all beauty, all excellence" (*Art and Reality*, p. 11). Or as he put it to his interviewers from the *Paris Review*, "The essential thing about James is that he came into a different, a highly organized, a hieratic society, and for him it was not only a very good and highly civilized society, but static. It was the best the world could do. But it was already subject to corruption. This was the center of James's moral idea—that everything good was, for that reason, specially liable to corruption" (*Writers at Work*, p. 60). That may be true for the earlier James— Cary especially admires *Daisy Miller*—but the later James is an austere comedian who stresses the toughness, not the fragility, of goodness. Maisie, Fleda Vetch, and Lambert Strether are all finally much tougher, much more durable than the corrupted people around them. True, at the end of their stories all three find themselves in stripped-down circumstances, but all three know by then that they can flourish in austerity, because each in his own way knows and values "the country of the blue." They neither need nor desire something static; rather, it is the corrupt, exploitative people they have dealt with, most of whom think of themselves as tough, who need cushions and who fear change. James is a deeply, marvelously, beneficently subversive writer; Cary, like many other readers, fails to see the radical purposes beneath the conservative surface of his work. The comic truth is that Cary is most in agreement with James when he thinks he is expressing his disagreement: "But my world is quite different—it is intensely dynamic, a world in creation. In this world, politics is like navigation in a sea without charts and wise men lead the lives of pilgrims" (*Writers at Work*, p. 60). Henry James knew New England well enough to recognize a pilgrim when he saw one; Maisie, Fleda Vetch, and Lambert Strether are all pilgrims.

It might have been easier for Cary to discover his agreement with Chekhov, but the plan of *Art and Reality* required him to draw all of his examples from novels. Certainly Chekhov had the same attitude toward mutability that led Cary to exclaim in a letter, "Change itself is my country" (*Joyce Cary: The Comedy of Freedom*, p. 1). That is the attitude that made Chekhov insist that *The Cherry Orchard* should be treated as "light comedy," much to the annoyance of his producers at the Moscow Art Theater, who wanted to produce it as "a serious drama of Russian life" (*Plays*, p. 29). *The Cherry Or-*

chard is about a group of people caught at a time of dramatic change in their lives. Some welcome it, some resist it, and some do both at once. They respond to the change ineptly, making themselves look as foolish as they really are; but most of them manage to adjust to the change reasonably well and at the end are ready to get on with the business of living the rest of their lives. The play is "serious" only to people who wish to deplore the fact that cherry orchards do not last forever, who wish to complain that it is not fair, not just. But Chekhov, like Cary and James and all other comic artists, knew perfectly well that the truly horrible fate for any human being would be to live in a world that did not change. A cherry orchard is a very small price to pay for release from the trap of what you are into the freedom of what you might become, even if it turns out, as it usually does, that what you become is not very different from what you were.

So much of this chapter has dealt with political issues that at least a little needs to be said about comic ideas of order. First, to state what should be clear already, comedy has no political preferences. It can thrive, has thrived, in societies with rigid class structures and autocratic government as well as it has in democratic societies that profess an ideal of classlessness, and it appears in at least some form in just about every culture known to man. Most of the comedians I have cited would be placed on the left by anybody laying out a political continuum, but that is probably a function of my own tendency to veer left rather than right. Certainly some very great comic artists stand on the conservative, right side of the continuum—Cervantes, Shakespeare, Pope, Swift, and Austen will do for openers. The only political order that comedy cannot stand is a totalitarian one because a totalitarian order attempts to suppress variety and to impose a single, univocal idea on every aspect of life. However, totalitarian states are not as efficient as they claim to be and comedy survives even in them, if only in the form of a few carefully phrased, cautiously whispered jokes.

Second, despite the fears of staid and nervous people, comedy is not anarchical. It is true that the Lord of Misrule is an important comic figure, but his reign is always brief and his subjects are never sincere in their loyalty. Also, there is much to be said for Orwell's observation that something is funny when it upsets the established order, but it must do it in a "a way that is not actually offensive or frightening"—that is, it must be only a temporary upset, not a permanent revolution. Anyone who stops to think calmly for a moment—though it is hard to do so when someone has just unloaded an irreverent joke on your most cherished ideal—will realize that comedy is too deeply attached to those things that themselves impose rhythm and order on human life ever to be truly anarchical. Moreover, if you savor the irrelevancies and foolishness in human affairs—and it is hard to think of a comedian who does not—you are bound to yearn for a society stable enough to give those qualities background and definition.

A valid description of the order that the comic vision cherishes cannot be stated in the language of politics, which is necessarily abstract and which ought to be logically coherent. The best indirect, symbolic description that I know comes from the notebooks of Renoir, in the passage that I quoted in chapter 2: "I propose to found a society. It is to be called 'The Society of Irregulars.' The members would have to know that a circle should never be round." Renoir was referring, of course, to the circles of art and lashing out at academicians who encouraged the use of the drawing compass, which Renoir considered the filthiest of all instruments. He thought that irregularity was the primary principle of the "grammar" of art, but as his son Jean shows in *Renoir, My Father,* a love of irregular circles carried over into every aspect of his thought. He hated the monotonous perfection of machine-made goods and furniture and loathed the notion of blending wines in order to make them the same year after year. He disliked the constraints and sameness of bourgeois manners, much preferring the roughness of peasant manners or even the arrogance of aristocratic ones because both leave room for individual variations. The concept of progress made no sense to him, partly because he knew so well the greatness of those who came before him, of Raphael and Rubens, and of the anonymous artisans of antiquity and the Middle Ages, but even more because he knew that the variety within the sameness of diurnal and seasonal repetitions was inexhaustible to anybody with the sense and the senses to examine it.

Renoir's paintings, especially the great late ones such as *The Bathers* of 1918, are direct, fully conscious explorations of the ideal of irregular circles. So, too, I think, are the films of his son Jean. *The Grand Illusion* and *The Rules of the Game* are the greatest of them; they are, among many other things, scathing critiques of societies that lock individuals into mechanical orderings of life. However, there is a great deal to be said for *French Cancan,* as frothy as it may seem to be. Jean describes it in *My Life and My Films* as "an act of homage to our calling, by which I mean show-business" (p. 269), but since the business of his hero, Danglard, is the making of shows (he is modeled on the founder of the Moulin Rouge), the fundamental subject of the film is "making." The term is defined in a passage earlier in his book: "Art is not a calling in itself, but the way in which one exercises a calling, and also the way in which one performs any human activity. I will give you my definition of art: art is 'making.' The art of poetry is the art of making poetry. The art of love is the art of making love" (p. 99). *French Cancan* is a celebration, not a glorification, of making. Danglard (played by Jean Gabin, who is so good that he does not appear to be acting, just as Jean Renoir is so good at filmmaking that even experienced reviewers can fail to notice how masterfully he is directing) cannot stop himself from making cabaret shows anymore than he can stop himself from acquiring mistresses; he does what he has to do simply out of the pleasant necessity to do it, with no concern for the economic consequences. The people around him, except for the bourgeois gentlemen who finance his shows and cheat him shamelessly, all respond to the need to make in the same improvident fashion. What little plot the film has focuses on the discovery by Nini, his protégée for the cancan show and sometimes his mistress, that she is someone who finds the making of the dance far more satisfying, far more necessary to her than any lover, whether he be an honest workingman, a Middle

Eastern prince, or even Danglard himself. All of this is brought together in the long, final scene in which Nini and the rest of the company perform their cancan in public for the first time. Our view of the dance, which is an astonishingly pure, joyous representation of vitality, is interrupted by only a few unobtrusive cuts to Danglard in a chair backstage, tense when the dance begins, then relaxing so much as its success becomes apparent that he cannot stop himself from swinging his legs in time to the music. Just before the end he comes out into the audience and there discovers a beautiful young woman whom you are sure he will make both his mistress and the central attraction in his next show.

As Jean Renoir learned from his father, making is a fundamental human necessity. "My father said of Mozart, whom he worshipped, 'He wrote music because he could not prevent himself,' to which he added, 'It was like wanting to pee' " (p. 99). Should anyone be disposed to doubt that making is that fundamental and that imperative a necessity, let him argue with Lynch and Koestler. Or even better, let him go into the caves of the Dordogne region in France and explain why and how our supposedly primitive ancestors of twenty thousand years ago made on the walls such elegantly stylized representations of the animals they hunted. A social order that is so constricted, so univocal in its structure and purpose as to interfere with man's need to make is precisely as perverted as one that would interfere with his need to "pee."

Orwell is right. A function of jokes, which themselves are a primary form of making, is to kick at the social circle to force it to leave room for making. A function—possibly *the* function—of comedy is to show us capacious, irregular orders of being in which we can be at home with all of our necessities, including the necessity to live with injustice as well as the necessity to make jokes about it.

CODA

In my preface I suggested that anyone writing about comedy would run into difficulties with general terms, and in the body of this essay I have proved my point, much more thoroughly than I wanted to. Jokes turn out under Koestler's analysis to be far more subtle and complex than most people think they are or want them to be. Comedy, as Lynch has shown, is not a relatively simple form for playwrights and filmmakers to work in but one of the primary modes of the imagination. It encompasses a very wide range of works, and I have been compelled to use the adjective *comic* in places where the common reader, whose good sense I do respect, never expected to find it. Needing a word for the fundamental perceptions of the comic vision, I found that neither *ideas* nor *meanings* would do and had to settle for the somewhat unfamiliar, and therefore not wholly satisfactory, term *images*. I had to agree with Lynch on the necessity of distinguishing between true and false comedy and comedians, though the odor of smugness about the terms *true* and *false* disturbs me. There is no adequate term for characterizing something as crucially important as the comic hero's way of responding to the pressures of reality; I had to speak of his *passivity* and suppress the urge to handle the term always with quotation marks. When I had to make a necessary, and surely obvious, distinction between the two kinds of comic heroine the best that I could do was to take the names of two great exemplars, the Wife of Bath and Pallas Athene, as labels for the groups. *Negligence* may be barely adequate for identifying the vital element in a comedian's attitude toward himself, but it is no more than barely adequate. And when I came to the inescapable issue of comedy's response to the injustice of the world I was at a loss for terms. To say, as I certainly had to, that the comic vision requires one to *accept* injustice may be profoundly misleading, and it does not do much for the cause of general understanding to term comedy's ideal of order an *irregular circle*.

Appropriately enough, I am most frustrated by the inadequacy of a generalizing term as I come to the end of this essay. I would like to finish by discussing for a few pages the simplest and deepest of comedy's images, the one that is so commonplace that every comic act discovers it and that therefore can be used to identify, if not define, works in the comic mode. I have called it the image of *play*, but that is only an approximate term and in common discourse it is easily misunderstood. In part the trouble is that in American culture we do not understand the concept of play itself very well; we tend to think of it as the opposite of work, as a kind of activity that may be relaxing and enjoyable but that is inherently trivial and that cannot serve any important purpose beyond the therapeutic one of helping people refresh their spirits. For many of us it is close to impossible to think of play as a way of doing that can be strong and reliable in the service of the most important aims we have.

But if the image itself cannot be named and discussed directly, the most important quality associated with it can be named and is well known to everyone who has ever wholeheartedly obeyed the imperative, Play!: gaiety. Play is usually artificial and always pointless in that it admits to no purpose larger than itself. (Observers frequently attribute larger purposes to play, but they are, I think, discovering uses for the skills involved in and developed by the play rather than perceiving purposes that control it.) Children's games offer clear examples. Even the infant's game of peek-a-boo has its "rules" governing where and how the adult may pop up on the child and determining the rhythm and intonation of his exclamations. The games of older children—the various forms of hide-and-seek and hop-scotch, for example—are always governed by elaborate rules, though they may vary considerably from neighborhood to neighborhood. To play the game the child must have sufficient gaiety of spirit to close out all other considerations while the game lasts, and the reward of the game is the increase of gaiety it brings in surges. No one is quite so gay—quite so fully, blissfully, heedlessly alive—as a child in the moment that he kicks the can and shouts, "All-y, all-y, in free!" The truly terrible injustice is that suffered by a child who is so battered by the circumstances of his life as to have no opportunity to play. That is Nabokov's point in the passage near the very end of *Lolita* in which Humbert Humbert recalls the moment that he stood by a mountain road and heard the sounds of children playing in a mining town in the valley below: "then I knew that the hopelessly poignant thing was not Lolita's absence from my side, but the absence of her voice from that concord" (p. 310).

As a society we are uncomfortable with gaiety; it is too pointless to trust, too effervescent to control. We prefer purposeful, deliberate, sensible ways of feeling. We convert play and games to contests so that we can count up winners and losers, glorifying the one and scorning the other; we demystify sex so that we can make that dizzying waltz an occasion for demonstrating technical skill; and we smother curiosity so that we can judge intellectual capacity by grade point averages and learning by degrees and publications. Fortunately, though, gaiety is nearly irrepressible, and it will leak through our most solemn efforts to banish it. Lovers with a comprehensive knowledge of the techniques cataloged by sexologists persist in discovering the goofy delight that the how-to sex books dare not mention, and scholars who have dutifully jumped all of the hurdles set up by a publish-or-perish system still gladly learn and gladly teach. Even athletes caught up in our most professionalized sports will insist on playing their games and relishing the gaiety they find in them.

For testimony to the power of gaiety—also for an extraordinary piece of American social history—see Lawrence S. Ritter's *The Glory of Their Times*. It is a collection of twenty-two interviews with old-time baseball players, most of whom flourished in the years before 1920, conducted by a man who is a distinguished economist and who is free of the clichés and concerns of sports writers. Every interview, without exception, glows with the delight these men felt in playing baseball in the big leagues. They played for money, of course, and some of them speak with relish of hard bargains they drove with the owners of their teams; but their wide-open secret is that they enjoyed playing the game so much that the money did not matter. Good as they were—a number of them are in baseball's Hall of Fame—it is not their own accomplishments they brag about, but those of the men they played with and against. And hard as they played to win—there is no point in playing a game if you do not play to win—they are as likely to talk about their defeats as their triumphs. What they loved was the feel of playing the game—of pitching, batting, and fielding in the company of men who could pitch, bat, and field as well as anyone ever has. Goose Goslin, who had over 2700 hits in 18 seasons in the big leagues, does not value the results so much as the hitting itself: "I truly loved those fast balls. Zip they'd come in, and whack—right back out they'd go." Sam Crawford, who got about 3000 hits in 19 seasons, tells with the greatest relish a story that hinges on the fact that no one, certainly not Sam Crawford or Ty Cobb, could get very many hits off of Walter Johnson when he was bearing down. Cobb, who was a mean, perhaps even psychotic competitor, could not stand the fact that his teammate Crawford got more hits off of Johnson than he did. What he never knew was that Crawford and Johnson were good friends. Johnson had the idea that Crawford's bats were lucky for him (like most pitchers he wanted desperately to be a good hitter, too) and Crawford would give him one whenever he wanted it. Consequently, when it would not affect the outcome of the game, Walter would slip him "a nice half-speed fast ball"; but he always took particular pleasure in striking Cobb out. Fifty years later Crawford was still chuckling to himself: "Cobb never did figure out why I did so well against Walter, while he couldn't hit him with a ten-foot pole" (p. 62).

Perhaps all that playful pride and delight is being driven from baseball by the money men who control the big leagues, but I doubt it. It still requires an extraordinary verve to play baseball well over a long season. That is a quality that cannot be either generated or controlled by any system of rewards and punishments; it can come only from the player's response to the game itself. Fans still attest to its presence, for they still applaud superb plays by members of the opposing team. Players still acknowledge it, as Cincinnati's Pete Rose did when he came to bat in the tenth inning of the sixth game of the 1975 World Series and said to Carlton Fisk, the Boston catcher,

"Isn't this a hell of a game!" That Cincinnati eventually lost the game when Fisk hit a home run in the bottom of the twelfth inning did nothing to change Rose's opinion; his pride and delight was in being part of the marvelously contested game, which was, by common consent, one of the best ever played.

Any sport worth playing is like a joke, just as any work of "making" in the arts or sciences is like a joke. The athlete must be completely absorbed in the playing of his game, just as the joker at the moment of making his joke must be so absorbed in his making as to be "absent" from the rest of the world. Both must act in full mock-seriousness, which is something very different from the desperate seriousness of someone trying to get out of a burning building. The desperately serious escaper does what he does with the best of ulterior motives, to save his life; the mock-serious athlete or joker does what he does essentially in order to do what he is doing. Often there are extraneous rewards for doing it that can be most impressive, but at the moment of doing his seriousness must be pure, it must be mock-seriousness. With that in mind, one might want to propose a category of the false athlete parallel to that of the false comedian: the false athlete is one who denies or fails to live up to the mock-seriousness of his game; whether he tries to convert it to a matter of desperate seriousness, as Ty Cobb did, or—what is much more common— he gets so aware of extraneous matters like money and reputation that he chokes. When true athletes fully live up to the demands of their game they demonstrate a great gaiety; that is why the rest of us go to watch them—to participate, if only vicariously, in that gaiety.

That is also, I think, our deepest reason for going to plays, concerts, museums, and libraries—to participate in the gaiety of artists. That is a fuller, much more complex gaiety because the artist's making is extended, as a rule, over a much longer period of time than the athlete's and because it always requires a fuller commitment of his resources and a graver exposure of his innermost self. A true athlete has to have the intellectual capacity to know and understand his game in remarkable detail and the spiritual strength to force himself to play it all out day after day, but still, his play is primarily a test of his physical abilities and courage. But the artist has to bring everything he has to bear on his making, all of his powers of intellect and imagination, all of his past, especially those parts of the past that most of us try to bury deep in unacknowledged dreams, all of his energy, and even, for musicians, dancers, painters, and sculptors, most of his physical abilities, too. A batter in the big leagues only has to stand up to big league fastballs; an artist has to stand up to the largest reality he is capable of imagining. And he has to do it with a seriousness that is as pure and impersonal as the athlete's and very nearly as urgent as that of the person escaping from the burning building. No wonder that there are so many commercial craftsmen and timid imitators in the arts and so few true artists. And no wonder that we come back again and again to the works of those few artists. "All things fall and are built again," says Yeats in "Lapis Lazuli," "And those that build them again are gay." It is not so much the meanings of works of art that we find inexhaustible as their gaiety.

The making of a work of art *is* like the making of a joke, even if it is a wholly somber and tragic work, and even if the artist finishes exhausted and broken. At the moment of making—at the time of shaping whatever the material may be into whatever form the artist is working in—there must be a gaiety that renders the artist heedless of himself and of all other considerations. That is the impersonal, objective element that lies at the center of art and is so completely baffling to univocal minds that cannot perceive objectivity unless the work parades its objectivity every step of the way. They want to know how something as deeply personal as a work of art can be considered objective, when they ought to be asking how an artist transmutes his own experience into something that resonates with the experiences of people separated from him by the barriers of time, nationality, class, sex, and race.

All art is a form of play. That is why we cluster around it, warming our spirits over its gaiety, cheered even by a great tragedy because it suggests that we, too, can find a way to unlock "the prison of our days" (to borrow a phrase from Auden's poem in memory of Yeats). But only comic art is *about* that image I have called play. That is comedy's special quality and gives it its special importance. If I were backed into a corner and forced to choose a single, simple, effective test for distinguishing the comic from the other modes of the imagination that would be it. Comedy may deal with all sorts of dark, disquieting material but finally it explores and celebrates the image of play. Noncomic art may deal in passing with that image but finally it concentrates on and celebrates something else. *Antony and Cleopatra* and *The Tempest* can serve very well to illustrate the distinction.

Antony and Cleopatra rings throughout with evocations of the power of sensual delight. One hears it most clearly in the great set-speeches—first in Enobarbus's lavish explanation to the Romans of Cleopatra's sway over Antony:

> Age cannot wither her, nor custom stale
> Her infinite variety: other women cloy
> The appetites they feed, but she makes hungry
> Where most she satisfies. . . .

And then in Cleopatra's lament for the dead Antony:

> I dream'd there was an emperor Antony:
> O, such another sleep, that I might see
> But such another man!
> His face was as the heavens: and therein stuck
> A sun and moon, which kept their course and lighted
> The little O, the earth. . . . His delights
> Were dolphin-like; they show'd his back above
> The element they lived in: in his livery
> Walk'd crowns and crownets; realms and islands were
> As plates dropp'd from his pocket.

It is not possible to create an eloquence equal to, let alone superior to, that of those speeches; a person who cannot learn from them the delight of giving full play to his sensuality is deaf to language and, I suspect, enfeebled in his sexuality. Moreover, these are not isolated evocations of the image of sensual play in the drama; its verse is so fabulously rich that even unstressed, throwaway lines evoke it memorably. "My salad days, when I was green in judgment." Or Cleopatra's sardonic comment on the pompous conqueror, Caesar: "He words me girls, he words me that I should not be noble to myself.'' And the swift reply of her attendant, Iras: ''Finish, good lady; the bright day is done, and we are for the dark.''

Yet, though *Antony and Cleopatra* is oddly close to comedy there is no doubt that finally it is a tragedy. It richly evokes, as it must, the image of play, but finally its concern is to measure again, and afresh, the tragic gap between human will and human reality. The passion of Antony and Cleopatra is fully willed as well as fully felt—they are no innocents surprised by the power of the currents they have fallen into. More important, they are fully conscious of what they are doing (though they may not be able to stop themselves from doing it) when they attempt to impose their passion on the world of empires and armies—they will themselves to be simultaneously passionate and imperial. They cannot succeed. Caesar must inevitably win the empire because his energies are purely focused on political schemes; he is so devoid of any impulse toward the passionate that the first time he comes into the presence of Cleopatra and her attendants he must ask, ''Which is the Queen of Egypt?'' Thus, the deepest note of the drama is sounded when Cleopatra prepares to depart from a world too paltry to accommodate a rule of passion: ''Give me my robe, put on my crown; I have immortal longings in me.''

The Tempest is every bit as complex as *Antony and Cleopatra*. One can scarcely argue that it comes close to being a tragedy, but it is so austere, so unflinching in its way of facing all of the issues of comedy, so unhesitating in its way of making demands of its audience that many viewers and readers are reluctant to classify it with the rest of Shakespeare's comedies or even to call it a comedy at all. Yet as poignant and as troublesome as it is in its naked insistence on accepting injustice and in its clear yet baffling assertion of our links with both Ariel and Caliban, *The Tempest* is unquestionably a comedy. Its deepest image is that of play, and it is most purely represented to us when Miranda first sees that miserable collection of traitors, ingrates, and drunks that accompanied her handsome Ferdinand to her father's island and exclaims, ''How many goodly creatures are there here! How beauteous mankind is! O brave new world, that has such people in't!'' *The Tempest* as a whole testifies that she is right. The beautiful, charming, innocent, empty-headed girl is

right. Even Prospero must resign all of his magical power and
knowledge and defer to her judgment, though, of course, it was he
who set the stage for her vision and judgment. And it is Prospero
who summarizes for us much of the wisdom to be derived from the
image: "We are such stuff as dreams are made on, and our little life
is rounded with a sleep." If we are made of such stuff, then it be-
hooves us to take ourselves and our world playfully, not seriously.
Take ourselves and it seriously, as the treacherous king and usurping
duke do, and we are in for nightmares in which nothing can be as it
seems to be. Take ourselves and it playfully, as Ferdinand and Miranda do by instinct and as Prospero does by hard-earned wisdom,
and we can be in for revels in which everything can be engrossing
because such possibilities abide in it.

It would be seemly to close this essay with one brief, strangely
magical evocation of the image of play. Any number of the songs
from Shakespeare's plays would do beautifully, but since I have
been discussing *The Tempest* one of Ariel's songs would be appropriate. Because Ariel is pure spirit play comes far more easily to him
than it can come to any human being. Lacking the human capacity
for feeling he can be blithe, while a human being, a Ferdinand, cannot help but sit on a bank "weeping again the King my father's
wrack." Nonetheless, what Ariel sings is true, for human beings as
for spirits. Reality will play with us, putting us through transforma-
tions that seem monstrous as long as we resist them but that can be
beautiful when we submit to them. Even death, that one transforma-
tion which most certainly, and most disturbingly, does await us all,
can be something lovely:

> Full fathom five thy father lies;
>   Of his bones are corals made;
> Those are pearls that were his eyes;
>   Nothing of him that doth fade
> But doth suffer a sea-change
> Into something rich and strange.

However, since I have argued throughout that the comic vision is
as much the possession of uncelebrated men and women as of great

artists, and since I suspect that this whole project started when my father took me to see a Marx Brothers movie when I was six years old, I will let my father, not Shakespeare, have the last word. A few days before he underwent his own sea-change he was visited by a young, nervous, naive priest. Thinking he would supply consolation for the impending event, the priest began gushing about the joys of being in heaven. My father took it as long as a true comedian could, but finally he had to cut off the gush. "Tell me, Father," he asked, "do they have flat races in heaven?" Not steeplechases or sulky races, which are scarcely better than no races at all, but flat races, with large thoroughbreds and small jockeys, which give a thoughtful man a reasonable chance of picking the winner.

I don't give any more of a damn about heaven than William Carlos Williams did, but if there is one, if they don't have any flat races there, the hell with it.

EDITIONS CITED

The citations within the text are to the following editions:

Berger, Thomas. *Little Big Man*. New York: Fawcett, no imprint.

Böll, Heinrich. *Absent without Leave*. New York: McGraw-Hill, 1971.

Cary, Joyce. *Art and Reality*. New York: Doubleday, 1961.

Cervantes, Miguel de. *The Ingenious Gentleman Don Quixote de La Mancha*. Translated by Samuel Putnam. New York: Viking, 1954.

Chekhov, Anton. *Plays*. Translated with an introduction by Elisaveta Fen. Harmondsworth: Penguin, 1959.

Cowley, Malcolm, ed. *Writers at Work: The "Paris Review" Interviews*. New York: Viking, 1959.

Freud, Sigmund. *Jokes and Their Relations to the Unconscious*. Translated by James Strachey. New York: W. W. Norton, 1963.

Hašek, Jaroslav. *The Good Soldier Švejk*. Translated by Cecil Parrott. New York: Thomas Y. Crowell, 1974.

Heller, Joseph. *Catch-22*. New York: Simon and Schuster, 1961.

Hemingway, Ernest. *A Moveable Feast*. New York: Scribner's, 1964.

Hoffman, Charles G. *Joyce Cary: The Comedy of Freedom*. Pittsburgh: University of Pittsburgh Press, 1964.

Huizinga, Johan. *Homo Ludens: A Study of the Play Element in Culture*. Boston: Beacon, 1955.

Ibsen, Henrik. *Six Plays*. Translated by Eva Le Gallienne. New York: Modern Library, no imprint.

————. *The Wild Duck*. Translated by Michael Meyer. New York: W. W. Norton, 1977.

James, Henry. *Stories of Writers and Artists*. Edited by F. O. Matthiessen. New York: New Directions, no imprint.

Koestler, Arthur. *The Act of Creation*. New York: Dell, 1967.

Lynch, William. *Christ and Apollo: The Dimensions of the Literary Imagination*. New York: Sheed and Ward, 1960.

McCormick, John, and Mairi MacInnes, eds. *Versions of Censorship*. Chicago: Aldine, 1962.

Mailer, Norman. *Genius and Lust: A Journey through the Major Writings of Henry Miller*. New York: Grove Press, 1976.

Mencken, H. L. *Happy Days*. New York: Knopf, 1940.

———. *Newspaper Days*. New York: Knopf, 1941.

———. *Heathen Days*. New York: Knopf, 1943.

Miller, Henry. *Tropic of Cancer*. New York: Grove, 1961.

———. *Big Sur and the Oranges of Hieronymous Bosch*. New York: New Directions, 1957.

Molière, Jean B. *The Misanthrope*. Translated by Richard Wilbur. New York: Harcourt Brace Jovanovich, 1965.

Nabokov, Vladimir. *Lolita*. New York: Putnam's, 1955.

Orwell, George. *Collected Essays, Journalism and Letters*. 4 vols. Harmondsworth: Penguin, 1970.

Renoir, Jean. *My Life and My Films*. New York: Atheneum, 1974.

———. *Renoir, My Father*. Boston: Little, Brown, 1962.

Ritter, Lawrence S. *The Glory of Their Times*. New York: Collier, 1971.

Silone, Ignazio. *Bread and Wine*. New York: Harpers, 1937.

Simenon, Georges. *Maigret's Memoirs*. London: Hamish Hamilton, 1963.

———. *The Little Saint*. New York: Harcourt, Brace and World, 1965.

———. *When I Was Old*. New York: Harcourt Brace Jovanovich, 1970.

Torrance, Robert M. *The Comic Hero*. Cambridge: Harvard University Press, 1978.

Twain, Mark. *The Adventures of Huckleberry Finn*. New York: W. W. Norton, 1962.

White, E. B. *Charlotte's Web*. New York: Harpers, 1952.

———. *Letters*. New York: Harper and Row, 1976.

Whitman, Walt. *Leaves of Grass*. Edited by Sculley Bradley and Harold W. Blodgett. New York: Norton, 1973.

Williams, William Carlos. *Selected Poems*. Enlarged edition. New York: New Directions, 1968.

INDEX

INDEX

200
INDEX

James, Henry (*continued*)
"The Next Time," 176–77; *Guy Domville*, 177; *Daisy Miller*, 178
Jokes: relation to comedy, 4, 17–20; role of aggression in, 5–6, 9–11; bisociation of matrices in, 6–10, 13–14, 16, 17; as creative acts, 7–8, 14, 16, 189–90; impossibility of universal appeal, 11, 14–15; role of rationality in, 11–12; role of familiarity in, 11–14; role of unconscious in making, 14–17; liberating power of, 16–17; relation to humor, 17–18; as a fundamental component of mental life, 19
Joyce, James, 56, 158; *Ulysses*, xi, 18, 47, 68, 101, 107, 124

Keaton, Buster: *The Navigator*, 3; *The General*, 3, 42–43; *College*, 42; as a true comedian, 42–43
Kenner, Hugh, 127
Koestler, Arthur, xii, 5–20 passim, 30, 38, 182, 185; *The Act of Creation*, xii, 5–20 passim, 125; *Insight and Outlook*, 5; *Janus: A Summing Up*, 5; "Jokes," *Encyc. Britannica* (15th ed.), 5

Langer, Susanne K., 24; *Feeling and Form*, 24
Lardner, Ring, 17, 47; "Haircut," 47; *You Know Me, Al*, 47; *Gullible's Travels*, 48
Lasch, Christopher: *The Culture of Narcissism*, 135
Laughter: and comedy, 3–4; a reflex, 4–5, 10; kinds of, 11

Laurel and Hardy, 11, 33
The Lavender Hill Mob, 8–9
Lawrence, D. H.: *Lady Chatterley's Lover*, 68
Lynch, William, xii, 20, 23–44 passim, 63, 66, 182, 185; *Christ and Apollo*, 23–44 passim, 75, 125; *Images of Faith*, 26; on "image industries," 26; *Images of Hope*, 29

Mailer, Norman, 135; *Genius and Lust*, 76, 79
Mann, Thomas: *Doctor Faustus*, 40
Matisse, Henri, 146
Mehta, Gita: *Karma Cola: Marketing the Mystic East*, 130
Melville, Herman, 88, 94; *Moby-Dick*, 71, 84–91, 99
Mencken, H. L., 136, 141–46; *The American Language*, 141, 145; *Prejudices*, 142–43; *Newspaper Days*, 143; *Heathen Days*, 143, 144, 145; *Happy Days*, 143, 144–45
Meredith, George, 37
Miller, Henry, 43–44, 62, 64–65, 68–69, 76–77, 79, 136, 138, 153, 163; "Defense of the Freedom to Read," 43–44; as a true comedian, 43–44, 48, 64–80 passim; *Tropic of Cancer*, 64, 68, 69, 76; relationship to transcendentalism, 65–67, 68–69, 77; *Sexus*, 66, 69; *Big Sur and the Oranges of Hieronymous Bosch*, 66, 76; "Obscenity and the Law of Reflection" (in *Remember to Remember*), 68;

INDEX